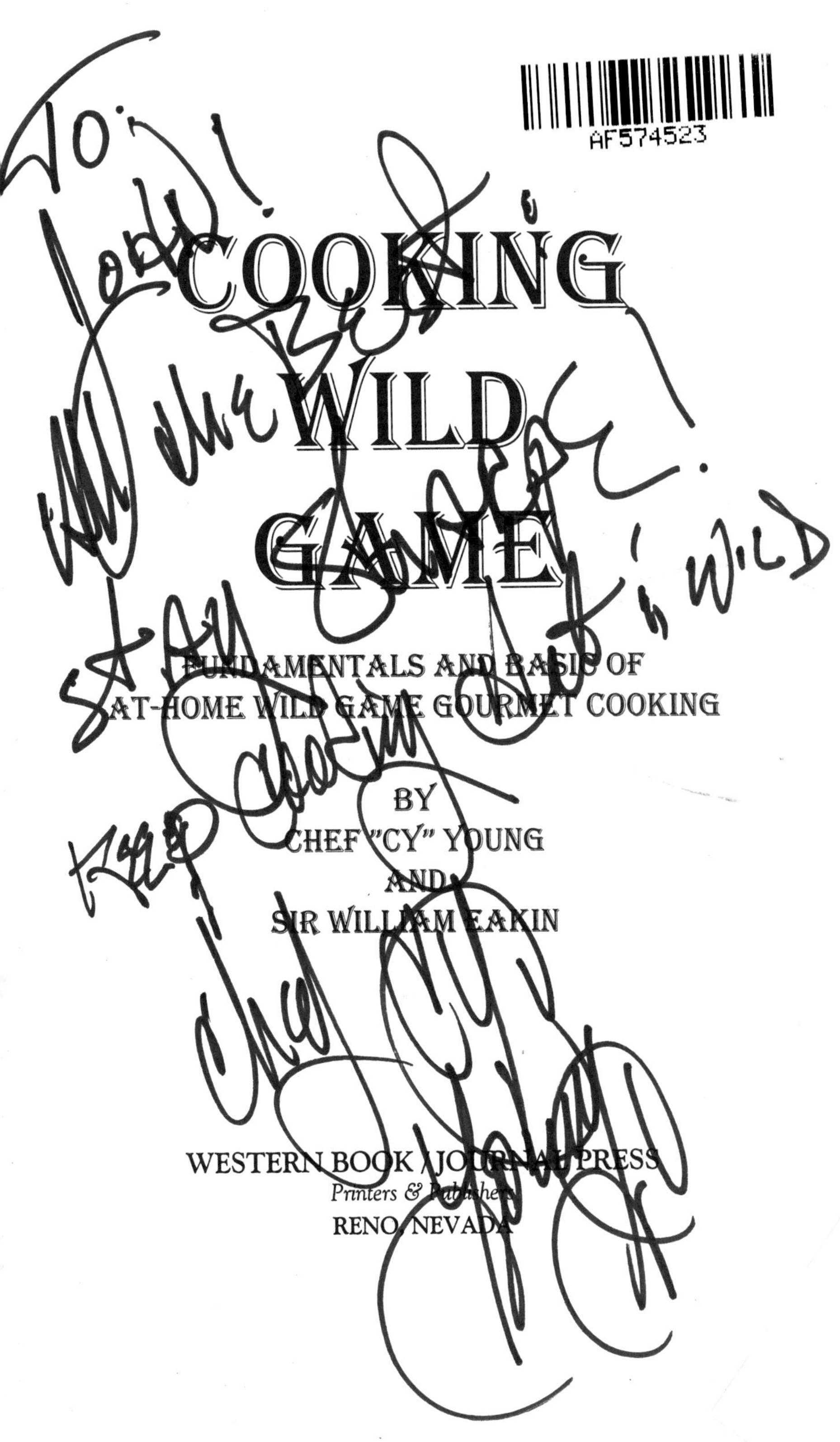

COOKING WILD GAME

FUNDAMENTALS AND BASIC OF AT-HOME WILD GAME GOURMET COOKING

BY

CHEF "CY" YOUNG

AND

SIR WILLIAM EAKIN

WESTERN BOOK / JOURNAL PRESS
Printers & Publishers
RENO, NEVADA

COOKING HOT! COOKING WILD GAME!

Fundamentals and Basic of At-Home Wild Game Gourmet Cooking

By Chef "CY" Young
Executive Chef
Instructor of Culinary Arts
Food & Beverage Consultant

& Sir William Eakin
A Knight of the Order of St. John Jerusalem
Member of Confederation Of Chivalry
Grand Commander the Military Order of Saint Steven
ANIC, BBA, MBA, Ph.D. , LL.D.
Diploma Oenology

ISBN: 0-936029-62-5
Library of Congress Control Number: 01-000000

Manufactured in the United States of America

Western Book/Journal Press
Printers & Publishers
Reno, Nevada

Volume I – The Name of the game is Wild Game!
www.smoothboarproductions.com

PREFACE

This book has some great wild game recipes in it and I aM the living proof. During the time the book was being written,I have gained forty pounds and four inches around the waist. I had to go out and purchase new shirts and pants because the old one got much to small. Every time I found a new recipe that I had not cooked I went into the kitchen and cooked it and ate, and ate, and ate. Oh it was good, but I did put on the pounds.

This book was written so that I would have an extensive group of recipes for cooking wild game. A friend of mine who is a hunter came home from a hunt with hundreds of pounds of deer. He called and ask if I would like some deer and I was more than happy to receive such a gift. I then went to look for wild game recipes and found none; anywhere. I have perhaps forty cook books and I found only two venison recipes in all those books. I went to a large book store that had perhaps three hundred different cook books and only a very few had wild game recipes. I then went to the internet and found only one brief reference to wild game cooking. In order to have enough wild game recipes for my own kitchen I realized we would have to write a book on the subject. Here is that book. If you have a good wild game recipe you would like to share please send me a copy. If you have suggestions on how to improve this book please let me hear your comments. EAT WELL.

Sir William Eakin

DEDICATION

To my life, my love, my wife, my Del'Ynda.
The beacon in my life from whom all my strength and blessings flow.

To Bill Eakin: Thank you for your vision your faith, your council and your support.

SPECIAL THANKS

There have been so many influences in my life that has brought me to this first book. I shall list only a few. For those friends, chefs, teachers, employees and colleagues who I have neglected to mention or thanked by name, you are not forgotten. You are remembered fondly and with many thanks.

To my Mom and Herman: You always said I could do this. Thank you for being there, always. You guided me down the right paths.

To my Brother, Carlton: You were my teacher, mentor, advisor, tutor, my big brother, and a friend. I can never say thank you, enough.

To Chef John Keglovitz: Thanks for being a tough chef, a great teacher, and a good friend during the hard times!

To my daughters, Kris and Alix. Thanks for being the daughters of a working chef, and understanding why I was not always there.

TABLE OF CONTENTS

INTRODUCTION 6

GAME! UNTO ITSELF, OR (WHAT EVER IT IS, I SHOT IT! CAN WE COOK IT? 12

GAME CUTS AND RECOMMENDATIONS 31

EQUIPMENT, TOOLS, AND DEFINITIONS 37

THE ART OF THE MARINADE 44

RUBING GAME THE RIGHT WAY: DRY RUBS 56

STOCKS! THE RICHEST OF ALL TASTES 72

SAUCES, GRAVIES, VINAIGRETTES AND TOPPERS 85

SMALL GAME, CRITTERS AND VARMINTS! 108

VENISON AND LARGE GAME 126

FISH & AND OTHER THINGS THAT SWIM 149

BIRDS ON THE WING AND IN THE OVEN 165

COMPLETING THE MEAL WITH SIDES! 182

DESSERTS TO DIE FOR 205

BREADS, ROLLS, BISCUITS, & BUNS 222

SALADS , GREENAND BUNNY FOOD 238

INTRODUCTION

We all have heroes in this world. My hero is Jed Clampett. I really liked Jed. Not until I grew older, did I appreciate the true character of Jed Clampett, and what he symbolized then, and what I miss about him now.

Every week, Jed would come into the family living room, in shadowed black and white, floppy hat, coon dog in tow, hefting that sleek smooth boar rifle. Every week, there was Jed, an anachronism from America's past. Jed reminded me of my dad, my grand dad, and the folks that went to my church. He was the farmer that drove by our house, at the break of dawn to work until dusk providing a living for his family. You bet Jed Clampett was cool. He was like us!

Every week Jed would heft that smooth bore "shootin at some food", and then he and his kin were off to Beverly Hills! Cement Ponds! Movie Stars! Country comes to the big city. What was it about Jed and family that I, so and many others still hold dear. Jed was the salt of the earth. He was good man. Honest, humble a hard worker who was thankful for what he had. He was a provider, a man who had little, but used all he had. Jed was a hunter, a shooter, a buck skinner, and a man who loved his wild game.

I remember Jed and Granny simmering some exotic pot of greens, or squirrel pie, hog jowls, boar on a spit. How we hooted and laughed! Every week we watched those "Beverly Hillbilly's" lament about not being able to find any thing worth hunting in California, and we laughed again.

Now, we jump to the present. I recently attended a reception for a new restaurant that is by far, an outstanding gourmet eatery. The Chef and his staff are very gifted in the culinary arts. Their presentation, balance and blend of flavors, use of color and seasonings are well above the normal fare you will find in most restaurants. What is ironic is that I was treated to such delicacies at $25.00 a plate as Wild Boar, Rabbit, Elk, Rattlesnake, Game birds, Squirrel, venison with sautéed greens and wild onions seasoned with garden herbs. Oh my God! Jed and Granny, you were cutting edge!

Wild Game has been a staple of the American family since the first Native Americans set foot across the land bridge eons ago. Those nomads who followed the great meandering herds of wild game into greener pastures, did not (I am quite positive) view themselves as trendsetters. Since our forefathers came to these shores, hunting, fishing and the taking of wild game have been as much a part of the American diet, and culture as apple pie or roast duck. The image of the noble buck, the mighty buffalo, the goose on wing, set against a cobalt blue, New England winter sky, is an integral part of our culture, our heritage, our America, then and now. If it were up to Benjamin Franklin, the wild turkey would have been our national symbol. The Bald Eagle would have been relegated to a less then favorable corner of American history. The question now arises as to what we would be carving on Thanksgiving Day. Would dad be carving a goose, a duck, and a buffalo? What to do with the leftovers, and those antlers!

As a Chef, I have seen many twists and turns in American culinary trends. I honestly can not count the comings and goings of what is "new" and what is "gourmet". I have seen many items touted and featured thru out the pages of the trade publications as the "new, hot food item" or trend. Within six months, we face a new battery of taste sensations, with a new gourmet trend, and so it goes. There are, and have been very few true food constants in this country. I have researched, explored, and culled many cookbooks, and recipes dating back to colonial times. Many hours have been spent "talking food" with chefs, cooks, old timers, ranchers and dirt farmers. After many years of research, I have reached the conclusion, as to the next hot trend on the American Culinary Scene. What we do not realize is that this trend has been with us for hundreds of years. Wild game has been the most understated, many times neglected, yet constant true American signature product that has withstood the test, and "taste" of time.

If I appear to be a cynic, who flaunts and waves the bloody shirt of disdain in the face of fellow chefs, then I am misunderstood. I have great respect for creative talent. I admire cutting-edge culinary skill. To become a chef, is to desire to rise to the top of your craft. To become a great chef means sacrifice, dedication, and great passion for your trade, long hours, little private time, and the daily endeavor to stay one jump ahead of the competition.

What I believe is that as we look to our culinary future, in many cases we have over looked the past. I have asked fellow chefs why wild game is not on their menus. Many have said that their customers equate wild game with, and I quote, "Rednecks with a six pack shooting Bambi", "Cruelty to animals", "need for more gun control", "I live in an area where you cannot hunt or fish", and the best quote, "I do not like the idea of eating anything that is part of nature, and has to be killed." Where do folks think prime rib comes from? A local store wrapped in plastic! I have yet been able to persuade a trout to hop out of a lake, role in seasoned flour, and jump into a sauté pan.

Do I advocate hunting? Yes, if you desire to do so. Do I advocate fishing? Yes, if you desire to peruse that sport. Can you purchase game in the middle of New York City? Yes you can. I am a firm supporter of new tastes, new ideas and new learning experiences. When it comes to foods and cooking, I am also a firm believer that most individuals have the potential to produce gourmet meals at home.

Wild game is, for most of the dining public, an undiscovered land, waiting, to be explored. There are countless textures and flavors that wild game-meats possess. There are degrees of flavor that will never be duplicated, in domestic meats, regardless of how you season the dish. We, as Americans live in a nation that has the greatest variety of both wild, native game, and domesticated game. We are blessed with the right to hunt and gather those game animals, and bring them home to our tables. If we do not choose to hunt and fish for our supper, then we have a growing market of suppliers that can provide us with any thing that our budding pallets desire.

What has driven me to write this book? As a Chef, a hunter, a teacher of culinary arts, and consultant, I am shocked at the limited degree of imagination, and recipes that are available to sportsman and those who like to gourmet cook wild game dishes. If I read one more recipe for venison chili, venison tacos, venison stew, I shall go mad! Imagine if there were only a few repetitive recipes on how to prepare beef, or chicken dishes! Imagine if you will, that every cookbook that you opened was a "rehash", (no venison hash, either), of the same old recipes. I was convinced a long time ago that wild game was a true gourmet delight. Due to poor presentation to the American public, misconceptions, and neglect by the mainstream, cooking establishment, wild game has been delegated to a side bar of high brow, over priced establishments. These establishments enjoy catering to those of sufficient taste and means. Wild game is not something that only people in doublewides in West Virginia eat. Wild game, and its preparation is a blank canvas, of limitless and unbound culinary potential, waiting for an individual artist to create their own masterpiece of signature art.

I want to assist you, the at home, wild game gourmet with a fresh approach to the preparation and cooking of wild game dishes. You will not find a collection of worn out recipes in this book. I have attempted to reduce classical gourmet techniques, methods and procedures into a simple set of explanations. This will allow you, at home, to create signature dishes that will become family gourmet favorites, using the most bountiful of natures gifts, wild game.

I would like to imagine Jed, Granny, Eli May and Jethro, dining at their billiard table. They have before them, such dishes as Venison Roulade, accompanied by a fresh Horseradish sauce. A field green salad, seared garden vegetables with a rosemary butter, home made yeast bread, hot and fresh from the oven, with fresh wild berry jam and fresh churned butter. For desert a light Lady Baltimore cake, with seasonal fruits and cream. After dinner, we cap off the evening with a short glass of aged whiskey, that Granny has been aging, down in the root cellar, as we listen to traditional mountain music, that is now in its re-birth.

Meanwhile, next door, the Drisdales are having another Fondue party, sipping stale martinis with canned olives, and eating some form of cock tail weenie, with green stuff and pimentos on crackers. Who is laughing now!

Jed, I really miss you. Y'all were ahead of your time.

Chef "CY" Young
Executive Chef
Instructor of Culinary Arts
Food and Beverage Consultant

CHEF "CY" YOUNG

GAME! UNTO ITSELF, OR (WHAT EVER IT IS, I SHOT IT! CAN WE COOK IT?

Wild game has been a continual food source for countless eons. Game animals have fed us, clothed us, and nourished us in both body and spirit. Early man followed migratory herds across the steps and plains of central Asia and Russia. They pursued the early bison, chased the wooly mammoths, and hunted the great stag and reindeer. Wild game provided the necessary nourishment and food source to early man that allowed primitive mankind the inner fuel to hunt, protect his family, to paint the walls of caves, to dream and reach for the stars.

One can imagine early man, returning from that day's hunt. His prey slung over his shoulder, triumphant, having brought home the necessary food to feed his mate, and his extended tribal family. As early man steps into the fire light, he throws the fresh meat on the floor of the cave and says to his mate, "Hey Honey, could y'all cook this thing up? I don't know what it is, but it looked tasty, and I got it with one spear. Could you do something different with this? That meat on a stick thing is gettin' kinda old. I would sure love ya if you would. You can keep the skin. I would like to help, but one of the boys just invented this thing called the six packs, and I wanted to keep working on that wheel thing. By the way honey, would it be ok if I hung this head on the cave wall, over there would look nice. Would y'all give a yell when the meat is ready? Love ya!

This was a great milestone in prehistory. It was then that early man created the need for a comprehensive and definitive cookbook for wild game cooking. It was at this same point in history that early women invented the sofa for early man to sleep on that night. There are moments in history that are repetitive. Modern man still brings home the game, hangs trophy heads on the walls of his abode, sleeps on the sofa on occasion, and both modern man and woman still have the need for a comprehensive, classical gourmet guide for game preparation and cooking at home. How some things never change, until now!

A wise and sage chef once told me that "If it has horns or hooves, and you drag it into this kitchen, I will cook you a dish that will make you cry!" Many hunters have professed similar thoughts. "If it is wild game, and you fix it just right, it will taste good, no matter how old, gamy, or tough." Other hunters have been a lot more selective in their opinions of what type of game you should take for the eventual trip to the dinner table. There are even a few chefs that I know who hold to the philosophy that, "All meat is protein!" With that concept of foods, I would assume that puppy would be considered the other white meat?

Wild game, unto its self, is unique. Each species has its own definitive taste characteristics, its own level of tenderness, its own degree of individuality. Wild or domestic game, game that is farm raised for commercial production and harvesting, unlike domesticated, commercial livestock allows a greater natural diversity in flavors, textures and gourmet culinary potential. Let us compare what is available to the American public in meats, both domestic and wild game.

The primary meats that consumers see displayed and purchase on a daily basis are beef, pork chicken, and fish. Out of the four major commercial meat groups, we have varying grades of beef. We have pork, whether it is ham, bacon, ribs or loin, pork is pork. For our feathered friends, we have chicken, turkey, Cornish game hen, and the occasional duck or goose. Fish choices, are usually the same, in most meat cases. There is salmon, trout, tuna, catfish, cod, white fish and shark.

Depending on your location and availability, there may be an occasional new breed of fish tossed into the mix. Crab, shrimp, scallops, lobster, clams and mussels round out the crustaceans, with the oddities (squid, octopus, frogs legs, etc) bringing up the flanks. If you look at the variety that we have to choose from, there are few choices from a culinary point of view.

Let us now examine wild game. There are in the continental United States, Canada and Mexico hundreds of individual and separate types of wild game, fish and fowl that are available to us to hunt, fish, or purchase. If you expand that number to include commercially raised game, the number is again expanded. Begin to count the number of exotic game animals that are available to us on the current specialty market, (the numbers grow yearly) the number of culinary possibilities has reached geometric proportions!

We, as sportsman, hunters, fishers, and gourmet consumers have at our disposal, a greater, more diverse potential then ever before in the history of cooking! Why are we not using this bounty in our kitchens?

Wild game, as a gourmet food, has been regarded by many potential gourmets, as nothing more then a carcass driven home over the hood of a car every fall. The link between hunting, wild game, and gourmet cooking is still a gray area that needs must be prodded forward into the bright culinary light. Wild game is no longer a narrow, culinary venue confined to hunters in plaid and camouflage. Wild game is available to all consumers to enjoy!

Wild game is predominantly gathered by individuals hunting and fishing, bringing home the yearly buck, doe, elk, pheasant, or quail. Fishing, is ranked among the top of national pass times, for not only recreation, but for providing a wide variety of game fish for the dinner table. Most states allow some degree of hunting, even if it is varmint hunting, year round. Sportsman and hunters truly have the opportunity to "shop on the hoof", which allows for a variety of great meals during the year.

What if you do not hunt or fish. What choices do you have to sample such sumptuous dishes as "Venison in Filo"? That solution is now available to the non-hunting consumer. Farm raised or commercially raised wild game meats are quickly on the rise. Most towns and cities have a specialty meats store, or meat distributor that has available, to the buying public a vast selection of "exotic" or domestically raised game for you to purchase. Restaurants, hotels, and fine dining establishments have been purchasing meats from these distributors for years. You did not think that Chef Joe, in the middle of New York, hefted his rife, and ventured into the wilds of Brooklyn to bring home the venison for his signature dish!

When did wild game fall from favor? It was when we, as consumers, became "civilized". Post World War II, the boom in American lifestyle, large commercial meat packing, production farming, the decline of open and rural land, all these factors prompted the decline of wild game on our table as a staple. It fell from grace, when many of us became to sophisticated to eat things that lived in the woods. Wild game became an unnecessary food item due to our new found prosperity. Consumers began to view wild game as a rustic food that our forefathers ate, because they had to. We kept very little of our culinary roots, (except the traditional Thanksgiving turkey). Folks raised in the country and rural areas had the benefits of hunting and fishing. These folks continued to enjoy the wild flavors of game and live a little closer to their roots. Over the past few decades, this has also declined.

I remember when milk was purchased from a neighbor who had dairy cows. Eggs were purchased from Mister Sam, next door. Hogs, chickens, beef, and lamb was either raised by our family, or purchased locally, on the hoof and processed by a local butcher. Wild game was gathered during season, and added to the freezer to supplement our family's dinner table. Vegetables, fruits, nuts, and other fresh delicacies were taken from our garden, and canned for the winter. I recall my mother, feeding a family of seven, for two weeks, on $60.00! That included the Ten Cent Comic that Mom bought at the store each week for me as a treat!

Then, we grew up, as well as our nation. It became easier to buy pre-packaged meats, chickens, pork, and adjust our diets for convenience. Cooking became more of a chore; mechanical devices and technology flooded the market with instant everything. Consumers demanded the best of instant everything! Why eat deer, when you can have steak and instant potatoes, with frozen peas, with you frozen pie, and quick bake bread? We have microwaves, PTA, soccer, MTV. Who has time to sit down to dinner? No one is home to cook! When we are home, we do not take, or make the time to prepare a decent meal due to "scheduling conflicts". When most individuals cook at home, meals are prepared as quickly as possible, with the most readily available of foods. Wild Game, its preparation and perception, as an acceptable dish does not fit into our schedules, or our conventional thinking.

As consumers, we purchase vast amounts of recipes, cookbooks and periodicals that take the same group of meats, fish and birds, vary their tastes with a sauce and seasoning and call the dish new. When we do not expand our culinary repertoire, and we relegate our dining to the same narrow selections of meats, or fare, we will no longer bother or attempt to reinvent so simple an item the wheel. By cooking wild game, you have the opportunity to not only reinvent the wheel, but you have the tools and products available to design an entirely new culinary vehicle!

Wild game cooking has blossomed into a new culinary age. With the resources and products that are now available to consumers, it is no longer necessary to "go a-huntin" to create wonderful wild game gourmet dishes. It is left to you, the at home, wild game gourmet cook, to set the standard. You no longer have to rely on a nuvue chef to tell you what is cutting edge. Create your own edge. Experiment, play have fun and most importantly, enjoy this grand culinary bounty, known as wild game! Do not bind yourself to the conventional realm of what has always been. If you are a hunter, or a non-hunting consumer, wild game cooking will allow you to enjoy an entirely new and exciting avenue of cooking, and dining! Bon appetite! Get hot, get cooking, get wild with game!

BASIC TECHNIQUES AND PREPARATIONS FOR DRESSING AND HANDLING FRESH WILD GAME

Beef is beef, chicken is chicken and wild game flavors are limited only to the taste of their own species, and variety! I have met so many folks who love to explain to me how they created a dish with venison that tasted just like beef! I ask them if it would not have been easier to have just shot a cow?

When you cook with wild game, it should be with the desire to dine on a dish that stimulates the palate. Wild game dishes should invigorate the taste buds, and allow you to create a new flavor that will provide you and your family with a simple, yet new gourmet dining experience! Wild game, by the virtue of its diversity, provides the greatest potential for culinary excellence. If you wish to take this great and abundant variety of flavors, and attempt to compact them into the same, conventional group as beef, chicken, or pork, then you need to read this book from cover to cover!

I will not attempt, (in any of my books) to provide you with recipes or suggestions that will detract from wild game flavors. I have never attempted to "convert" a wild game dish to domestic flavors. I believe in savoring the true taste of what you prepare and cook. If you desire to have a dish "taste like chicken", then cook a chicken. A chef I might be; a magician I am not.

There is an old saying that states "Opinions are like belly-buttons, everybody has one". This rule applies to the care, field dressing, and cleaning of fresh killed game. I am not going to jump into this debate. Each hunter, fisherman, guide, and sportsman has his or her own way of handling their kill. I am only going to emphasize a few basic safety rules for handling you fresh game kill. If you wish to use a pocketknife to process your game, and it works for you, then God Bless! I am not about to tell you how to hunt your game, just how to make it taste great! I want you to handle your game in a safe and prudent manner from a "chef's perspective".

The first technique or suggestion is the most basic of all principles. If you wish to have meat that is safe and good to eat, then perform proper cleaning and storage in the field. This obviously does not apply to those folks who purchase their game meat from a store or supplier. I will advise those who hunt to go prepared to the field with those items of equipment that will allow them to clean, store and transport their fresh game in a safe and secure manner. I have seen many hunters who will do the least amount of field dressing necessary, then throw their deer into the back of their truck for the long drive home. You would not want to eat beef, chicken or pork if were handled this way. Why treat your fresh game in this manner?

You should bleed the kill immediately. I carry a pocket block and tackle lift that allows me the mussel to lift the deer for field dressing. Remember to cut with care. You do not have to perform surgery on you kill, just exercise care when cutting. You do not want to cut into the entrails, intestines or other body organs that will contaminate the meat. Many hunters prefer to remove the scent glands first. I leave this option up to the individual. I prefer to remove the scent glands first, using a short bladed, highly sharpened fillet knife. I also carry a small amount of water, and clean the blade thoroughly after each gland is removed. You do not wish to "drag the scent" onto other parts of the meat.

If you wish to save the heart, kidneys, tongue or liver, then do so, using care in their removal. Many elk hunters discard the liver, as elk liver tends to be contaminated with liver flukes, and may cause illness. Wrap these organs in cheesecloth, and place them into a plastic bag and pack on ice, after allowing the organs a short time to cool. Place the organs into a small ice chest for transport home. Be sure to wipe the body cavity thoroughly, with a few damp cloths, then dry, with clean cloths. Allow the game to cool before cutting and bagging.

I have been with hunters who will use a few hands full of grass, or a pocket rag to wipe down the body cavity. Do not do this! You do not know what bacteria or contaminates are on the grass or foliage. Apply this principle to the wipe rags. I saw a hunter wipe down the body cavity with a cloth that he had used the day before to remove excess oil and dirt from his rifle, and had forgotten that he had done so. Use common sense and caution when handling your fresh game.

Large game should always be dressed and skinned as soon as possible. Remove any damaged tissue from around the shot or wound area. I use a strong salt and water "soak solution" to remove any excess blood from around the wound. Look for bone fragments, and remove them from the wound area. I also field cut my game into smaller sizes for transporting. Large, clean plastic trash bags are great for transporting game. I also invest in "waxed boxes". These containers are the commercial type that meat producers use to ship meat and poultry in. These boxes are constructed to hold ice without leaking, and will provide insulation that will keep your game at a stable and safer temperature. Ask you local butcher, meat processor, or grocery store if the have any to spare. These containers are also used to ship fresh produce on ice, and my local grocery store has never minded giving me a few around hunting season. If the waxed boxes were used for produce shipping, I simply rinse them out with water, towel them dry, and store them until my next hunt.

It never hurts to invest in some ice to transport your game. You always want to prevent as little spoilage and bacterial growth as possible. Icing down your fresh kill while transporting is only common sense. If you do not have anything available other then plastic or bags available, then use those. You would not allow steaks, or a roast to ride in the back of your car without refrigeration, so apply this same logic to your fresh game.

For small game, cut, gut, and skin as soon as possible. Remove the head feet and tails, and skin. Allow your small game to cool, and wrap in cheesecloth, and wax paper. Ice and transport as soon as possible to prevent spoilage.

If you hunt "critters", such as opossums, raccoons, then you want to allow the carcass to "rest" for 24 hours before skinning. The skins of these animals are a bit more difficult to remove. I suggest that you refrigerate them, after cleaning and rinsing, then skinning. Woodchucks, as an example require that the glands be removed immediately, as not to leach any nasty flavors and toxins into the meat. Rattlesnakes should be decapitated at least six inches behind the head. The rattlesnake should be cleaned immediately, with care given during the gutting and skinning process. Please remember to bury or cover the head of the snake after decapitation!

Check with any local hunting or sporting store in your area for suggestions and tips for local game cleaning techniques. I would suggest a little before hand knowledge of what you are hunting, and how to process what you shoot. I am currently researching a book on the processing of all North American game. This will be of great assistance to all hunters and sportsman, and will include a more definitive explanation for you to follow. For the time being, I am simply touching on a few basic highlights and suggestions!

Many hunters wish to age their fresh large game kill. There is a vast difference of opinion as to what technique is the best. You should remember that aging, hanging, or flavoring of wild game meat is simply allowing bacteria to "break down" the tissue and begin the decomposition process. Natural bacteria begin to tear down the meat fibers, allowing the inherent flavors in the tissue to begin to alter. If you are familiar with aged beef, and what a high degree of flavor and tenderness it has, then you will want to age your fresh game for a few days.

My suggestion is that you do not simply "hang" your kill in the carport, and allow it to begin to decompose. I would attempt to find a processor or butcher that would allow you to age your beef in a temperature controlled cooler for a few days before processing. Your game should be allowed "hang" in a stable, constant temperature setting, (about 40 degrees) and not become exposed to any possible contamination from outside sources. Freezing will also flavor, age and tenderize the meat. I do not prefer this process as it tends to "tear down" the tissue in to dramatic a manner. One point should be agreed upon regarding aging your game meat. If you desire to achieve a more beef-like flavor and quality, then definitely age your game meat.

Regardless of which method you prefer, you should always be aware of safety, and proper handling of raw meats, fish or fowl. If you process game at home, then have available some of the tools and equipment that I have outlined in that chapter. I would like to remind those home gourmet hunters and cooks to hold on to the bones, and bits of meat that are normally discarded. You will want to retain them for your stocks. Rinse, cut, wrap and freeze them until you are ready to produce your fresh game stocks. Freezing will not detract from the flavors and tastes that are produced during the stock making process. Freezing will lock in and stabilize the natural game flavors, which are released during the stock making process. Remember to wrap and seal the bones well, prior to freezing to prevent "freezer burn".

Large wild game meats are by nature, very lean. Wild game does not carry very much fat, (depending on the spices), and require a process of reintroducing fat to the meat know as larding. Larding of game meats is a very simple process.

If you are going to cook a roast, for example, you will wish to have available a small amount of bacon, salt pork, or similar fat. I have a friend that has his local butcher save his beef and pork fat trimmings. He then uses these trimmings, to lard his game, and it does not cost him a dime! The larding process is done before the game is placed into the marinade. Make a series of small, ½ to one-inch deep cuts or incisions in the meat. Using a dull, table knife, push or insert small, thin cuts of fat into the meat. Lard the meat evenly to insure that there is equal, and ample fat to cook into the meat. During the cooking process, the fat will absorb into the game tissue, adding adequate fat for the cooking process. It is up to the individual cook as to what type of fat or flavors he or she wishes to impart to the meat.

Small game is usually treated in the opposite manner from large game. Small game has a tendency to retain more of a fat layer. In this fat layer is where the concentrated flavor of small game "accumulates", giving some small game a particular strong, and "wild" flavor. Several species of animal that have a very strong game flavor due to their fat are beaver, woodchuck, raccoon, opossum and porcupine. You will want to immediately cut and trim as much of the fat from the animal after shooting. A hunter once told me that he would rub a large hand full of baking soda on the cleaned and dressed small game, and then rinsed it clean in cold water. He said that this aided in removing and neutralizing a lot of the "hard and strong" game taste.

By far, squirrel and rabbit have the least of this wild, "fat flavor". This is why rabbit and squirrel require less marinating and seasoning to decrease the wild flavor of their meat. Secondly, rabbit and squirrel require less seasoning, and will offer the at home game gourmet a vast opportunity to use these two game animals in a wide and diverse variety of new and exciting game dishes. Rabbit and squirrel flesh is the game meat most commonly referred to as "tasting like chicken". I would disagree, except to say that these two game meats "cook" as well as chicken, and have the most creative flavor potential, as chicken does. As far as taste, both have always tasted like rabbit and squirrel to me!

Game birds possess the most delicate flavors of any wild game. It does not matter if they are waterfowl, or upland game species, game birds are a true gourmet's friend in the kitchen. If there is one piece of advice that I may offer to those who hunt, it is to take the time to clean, dress and chill your fresh kill as quickly as possible in the field. Game birds will begin to go south very quickly. Most of the time, a bird is shot, and tossed into a game bag, or carted around half the day in less then favorable conditions. I can not stress enough the importance of quick and speedy preparation of fresh wild game birds or waterfowl. A game bird's flavor will alter in a very short period of time, there by rendering a less the favorable flavor to the meat.

My solution is that you maintain or have close at hand a "bird cleaner" or "duck plucker" who will begin to clean and process the game birds, as they become available. This is a thankless job, but a chore that will almost guarantee the best tasting results by far. Another solution is to set up a preparation table with all the necessary items to field dress your birds as quickly as possible. Allow your fresh kill to cool or chill quickly. When you are hunting, use an open mesh bag to allow the birds to cool rapidly.

Remember to bleed the game birds as you would a fresh killed large game. Exercise the same care in cleaning and removing the organs. I always carry a few pair of disposable rubber gloves with me, to prevent cross contamination should I have to "get my hands messy". It only requires a few minutes to field dress a bird, but it is worth the expenditure in time and effort. Always make the effort to have suitable ice and a cooler ready to place your fresh game in, and prepare to transport home. As soon as time permits, clean your birds fully and carefully, and prepare them for freezing. The added effort will pay off in the kitchen later!

Fish are the quickest and (at times) easiest to clean, maintain and transport. My suggestion for fish is to behead, descale and gut as soon as possible after catching, and pack them on ice as soon as possible to complete the cleaning and dressing process in more comfortable surroundings. It is up to the individual as to preferred cleaning methods. I always attempt to have a good fillet knife at hand, as well as a roll of plastic wrap and plenty of ice. I can say in all honesty, that by taking a little time for preparation, I have never had any fish that I have caught go bad!

Some fish have a stronger and more "grand" flavor then others. I have had some folks tell me that they do not like fresh trout because it has a "fish flavor". Others prefer the more delicate of salmon. While others still prefer the rich and workable taste of fresh catfish. The choice is up to the individual pallet. I enjoy almost all fish and seafood. I have one suggestion. Try to prepare your game fish as many ways as possible. I have offered die-hard catfish haters a "new taste treat", and they have loved it! Only to find out that it was the dreaded catfish!

Cooking wild game or game fowl is very similar to cooking beef, chicken or pork. The difference being availability. Do not let a preconceived idea or notion about wild game set you off, of partaking or delving into this area of culinary, or gourmet dining.

Large game is usually prepared and cooked as you would a similar cut of domestic beef. Small game and game birds are normally prepared as you would chicken. How you cook your goose, or game as the case may be, is entirely up to what recipe you choose, and what type of game you are cooking. If you are a great home cook, and can produce a fine meal using domestic meats, then you should are ready to become a great at home, game gourmet cook!

Seasoning wild game is a developed art form. As each individual has there own likes, dislikes and tastes, we all have common agreements as to what tastes good, with what. I have attempted to combine herbs, spices and seasonings that will complement the flavor of specific game dishes. Certain herbs will enhance the flavor of particular game animals. If you are one of those individuals who automatically piles salt and pepper on to every thing that they eat, then I would urge you to try the seasonings that are coupled with the game recipes first. You may be pleasantly surprised! Spices, herbs and seasonings are blended and designed to balance, enhance, finish of increase a dish's taste. Seasoning never should be used as a mask. As you begin to branch out on your own cooking adventures and experiments, please bare in mind that most book stores have inexpensive spice and herb books in stock. I would invest a few dollars and acquire a copy of a guide to cooking spices and herbs. A book such as that will give you a better understanding of how and why particular seasonings and herbs work and taste. Never be afraid to push out the envelope, and construct your own variations of seasonings and herb blends.

A technique that I have used for years is to make a test batch of seasonings, and taste them. Get the raw taste first, and then test cook a small piece of game with that seasoning. Most if not all professional chefs use this tried and true "test flight" technique to perfect a taste. Experimentation is half the fun, as well as getting to eat the mistake!

Marinating is very important when working with game. Many game animals have a strong, gamy taste, and most folks do not enjoy that pungent a flavor to their meats and birds. This is why marinating is very important in preparing wild game for cooking. I encourage you to read the chapter on marinades and rubs to get a deeper understanding as to the techniques of marinating and rubbing wild game the correct way. I will say again that at no time do I use a seasoning, a marinade or a rub to bury the natural game flavoring of a particular game dish. I use these marinades, seasonings and rubs to enhance and bring forth the unique and distinctive flavor in the wild game dishes that I prepare.

A CHEFS PERSONAL CONCEPTS AND PRINCIPLES

This short, yet most personal section, I felt compelled to add to this cookbook. This is a chef's nickel's worth of advice on the art of cooking, and kitchen philosophy. When I decided that it was time to write this cookbook, I wanted to convey to both the novice, as well as the "seasoned" cook, a small portion of what makes any cook, truly good. A fellow chef once told me what he felt made an individual great in the culinary arts. He said that it was the ability to perform the most basic and rudimentary of chores to the best of our ability, consistently, and with passion, day in and day out! "If you loose your passion in cooking, then everyone will taste it!" Cooking is not hard! Individuals make it hard! There is no secret to becoming a great cook. Like everything in life, if you wish to become skilled or proficient in a particular area, then embrace it with vigor, and practice, practice, practice!

Whether you have ever prepared a wild game dish before, or if you are only familiar in cooking domestic meats, the basic practices and principles are the same. Do not let the fact that wild game is uncommon as a cooking medium bother you. All domestic creatures were wild at some time in their ancestry. Chickens, cows and pigs were not created with a browning bag and set of cooking instructions. Therefore, any qualms that you might have about getting wild in the kitchen should fall by the way side.

Here are a few concepts and principles that I have always applied to cooking, and several leads for you to follow for dealing with wild game dishes. First, follow the recipes, directions and tips presented to you in the cookbook, as these instructions are created as a guide that will allow you to prepare a specific dish. When you have become familiar with cooking wild game, then you will begin to add or subtract from the recipes as to personal tastes.

I also recommend that you view wild game cooking as a series of "block stacking exercises". Read the recipe, and outline your order of ingredients, equipment, and procedures before beginning the actual cooking process. Wild game preparation and cooking is more involved then preparing a dish with domestic meats. The results are equally worth the effort. Stack the blocks, in proper order, and you will do fine. If a recipe or procedure is new or unfamiliar, do not let it bother you. I can tell you horror stories for hours on end about my first attempts cooking a new game dish, or developing a new game recipe. Mistakes will happen. Just remember, it is only food.

Next, I recommend that if specific questions or problems do arise that you consult the chef's best friend, "The Joy of Cooking". Every chef that I have known has had a copy of "Joy" floating around his or her office or kitchen. If you are a novice cook, or feel that you lack the necessary experience to tackle complex cooking, then Joy of Cooking is your best bet at understanding basic principles and concepts for cooking. Joy of Cooking has undergone some revisions in recent years, and if you search your local second hand book shop, try to find a copy that was produced during the 1970"s or before.

Do not be afraid to have fun with your cooking. I find cooking to be relaxing, and at times, almost therapeutic. Cooking at home allows you, the at home, budding game gourmet cook to unleash your creative side. Producing a great final product will not only garner praise for the cook's accomplishments, but will provide you with a meal to be shared and enjoyed by all. Cooking wild game, or any dish allows a degree of hands on interaction with natures most basic of ingredients. As there is life in bread, there is a degree of pleasure unbound in preparing a truly great and gourmet meal.

My fundamental concepts for cooking are simple. There is no chore in cooking. The only tasks that are necessary are that you buy the food, you cook the food, serve and eat the food, and bask in the dining experience. All other steps and procedures involved in cooking, are a pleasure and a joy! Many of my fondest memories as a child, thru adulthood, have been at the dining table, with my family, friends or customers. There are few professions or chores in life that will produce as an immediate or recognized response as cooking a superb meal. Enjoy your creation with family and friends.

Keep cooking simple. Do not read so much into the procedures and steps as to escalate the act of boiling water into a state dinner. I have had a number of beginning cooks complain that a particular procedure or concept was hard to understand. I always tell them that in cooking, as in all things in life, you are in a learning process. Work at what is difficult! Relish what is simple! Do not expect to walk into a kitchen and be the next food sensation over night. Learn the basic skills, learn to apply them, and grow a little with each new dish or recipe you attempt. Perfection in the kitchen is always desired. Perfection in any kitchen is rarely achieved. Ask any veteran chef if he has ever burned bacon. If he says "Never", then run for the hills, he lies!

Treat cooking as a learning experience. Cooking has been around since OG the caveman discovered that meat on a stick was a lot better tasting then Wooly Mammoth Sushi! The history of Chefs, and cooking dates back several thousands of years. Learn the twists and turns of what and why we cook the food's we do. You will not only be impressed at the degree of knowledge that you gain, but you will never run out of table conversation as you are feasting on that gourmet meal you just produced!

It never fails to amaze me, as to the amount of fuss and bother that people profess about cooking a meal. Cooking seems to be the last task that anyone wishes to perform. A chef I knew from Europe once told me that "In America, you have the greatest of everything! However, you have forgotten to appreciate the small things. You do not dine, in America. You eat! You do not enjoy your food, you hurry and you run on to something else! The family meal and good cooking is not something to be scorned. It is to be loved and enjoyed, practiced and proven." Amen, to that, brother!

As you now begin a new chapter in home gourmet cooking at home, remember that skills in cooking, like adventures, are sometimes gained in small steps. This is so true in food. Go now and start a grand adventure!

GAME CUTS AND RECOMMENDATIONS

A fare number hunters and sportsman have their fresh large game processed at a local butchers or game processors facility. The positive side of having a "professional" process your fresh kill are many. First, he has the equipment to properly render and cut the meat. He can provide to you the proper cuts of meat, sausage, and ground meat in a clean and safe manner. The game meat usually comes back to you in white butchers paper, marked and ready for the freezer.

Second, the meat processor will render the meat in a clean and safe environment, which will greatly reduce the potential of ending up with some form of contamination.

Third, your butcher or game processor is more likely to spot a potential problem with your fresh kill then you. He sees a lot more game in a season then you may ever see in a life time. Many game processors and butchers also know the best way to process a large game animal to provide the most amount of useable game meat. I would check out your local phone book to find out which butcher or processor in your area handles wild game, and contact them for pricing and details.

For those of us who have dealt with game animals and have been cooking them for years, we have a fair idea, as to what cuts of game we enjoy, and what we eat the most. What of the non-hunting game novice? Allow me to provide you with a brief understanding of large game, venison and its various cuts and uses.

Venison is not just "deer". Venison is considered any antlered member of the deer family, to include moose, elk, and caribou. The most common, and therefore the most accessible wild game meat or venison meat is that of the Whitetail, and the

Mule deer. Whitetail deer are found throughout the United States, Canada, and venture as far south as into South America. Mule Deer are found predominantly in the Western part of the United States, form Canada, south into Mexico.

The Mule deer is a heavy, muscular deer, which will provide a bit more meat then the Whitetail. Whitetail deer will usually field dress out at around 125 to 150 pounds. The mule deer will field dress out at 175 to 200 pounds. Not a bad amount of meat for the freezer. How do we select our cuts and choices of meat? What if our neighbors ask us, Hey! Would you like some venison? What if your neighbor shows up with a few pounds of ribs and backstrap? What to do now!

Normally venison is divided into 10 areas or primal cut zones after it has been cleaned and skinned. These cuts and recommendations for cooking use are as follows:

1. The Hind and the Fore Shank. This meat is primarily used for soup meat, stew meat, ground meat and sausage.
2. The Round. This area is used for the steaks, and steak cuts.
3. The Legs. This area will provide you with roasts.
4. The Loin. Loin cuts will also provide you with roasts, and choice cuts such as "porterhouse, sirloin and additional steaks".
5. The Shoulder or Chuck. This area will provide both ground meat and shoulder or pot roasts.
6. The Rump. This area will provide very nice pot or rump roasts.
7. The Flank and Breast. This area will provide additional meat for soups, stews, ground meat, and sausage.
8. The Neck. The neck are will provide additional stew meat or ground meat. A point to remember. The neck area has a good number of tendons that must be removed before processing.

9. The Ribs. The ribs will provide a fine meal for Bar-B-Queing, or oven baking
10. The Back Bone or "Back Strap". Considered by many to be the best cut of the deer. I reserve this meet for my Venison Fajita Recipe.

These are the primary areas and uses for venison. If you dress out an elk, and have it processed; you will have roughly the same cuts of meat, just a lot more in volume. It is usually agreed by most hunters, that elk and moose have the closer taste to beef, then any other game animal. If have found that this does hold some truth. Moose and elk have a comparable flavor that is similar to beef, however, do not expect these game animals to be a cow in wild game disguise.

Big game meat is different in that you have a broader variety of game such as bear, mountain goat, mountain, or Big Horn Sheep, Wild Boar, antelope, and Buffalo. Antelope is closer to the mountain goat in ancestry then to the venison or deer family, and is usually listed in the big game family by most sportsmen. Antelope meat is very close to venison, but needs a bit more work to produce a good flavor and tender consistency.

Big game is in many cases is more difficult to prepare. Bear can either be a disaster, or a delicacy. Bear requires care in both preparation, and cooking. Bears are omnivorous creatures. A bear's meat will "season" or flavor depending on its diet. The quality of its meat will also depend on the bear's available food source. The bear's fat holds the majority of the game flavor, and must be removed to avoid the strong and very unpleasant wild flavor. It has also been debated as to when bear meat tastes better, before or after hibernation. Wild Boar also can produce fine meat, but should be prepared with care. Wild Boar are also omnivores. What ever a boar eats within a twenty-four hour period prior to its demise, will flavor the meat. The smaller, southwestern cousin of wild boar, the

Javelina is considered small game. The Javelina ranges between 40 to 60 pounds. It produces a meat that is "pork-like", but lighter in texture and taste. Javelina actually produces a finer Bar-B Que, then its larger cousin, and the wild boar.

Both wild boar and bear share one common problem that should be addressed when preparing and cooking this wild game meat. Trichinosis, which is a parasite, is commonly found in both bear and boar. Proper preparation and cooking to an appropriate temperature will resolve this problem. Freezing will also aid in eliminating this parasite. It has been recommended that these meats be frozen at a temperature of minus 10 degrees or lower, for at least a month or longer. Does the freezing process work? I would not bet the farm on this method. I would highly recommend that you cook these game meats to at least 150 degrees, internal temperature or higher to insure that the trichinosis parasite is eliminated.

Of all the North American, big game animals, mountain sheep is considered by many to be the best tasting, and will produce some of the finest flavored meat. Big game hunters have attested to the tender quality, and excellent taste of this game meat. The quality of any game meat depends on the age of the animal, its diet and general health. The younger and stronger the animal, the better quality of meat. If you ever have the opportunity to taste "mountain Sheep", I am sure that you will agree that it is truly a "wild game gourmets delight"!

We come to the largest game animal that is now domestically raised and produced in North America, the Buffalo. The buffalo was once the staple meat animal of the North American Plains Indians. Vast and wondering herds of these animals once provided meat for millions of western bound settlers, migrants and American Indians. Buffalo is now commercially produced on ranches, but buffalo hunts still occur, usually by raffle or for a hefty fee. Buffalo meat is absolutely the finest of game meats. It has the quality of prime beef, with a finer texture. This fine meat texture allows you the opportunity to slow roast or smoke buffalo meat, which produces a superb product. Buffalo meat will also absorb and marry in most flavors, (as dose beef) which allows you a limitless amount of variations, recipes and flavor possibilities.

Game birds and water fowl may be processed and treated as you would their domesticated cousin, the chicken. Game birds and waterfowl are usually retained whole until they are ready to cook. Game birds and waterfowl may be cooked whole, halved, quartered, eight way cut or breast only. It is entirely up to the individual cook and the recipe as to how the bird is prepared

Smaller game birds, such as quail, grouse, chukar, snipe and woodcock, are usually cleaned, and retained whole until cooking. Smaller game birds may be prepared, as are larger birds.

Larger waterfowl, and game birds such as goose, pheasant, sage hens and wild turkey should be treated the same as other game birds. Fast field preparation and cleaning will allow a superior taste, and reduce the chances of your birds "going south". I was recently asked as to the best way to sore game birds in the freezer. My solution is to save as many 2 liter soda bottles, and ½ to one-gallon milk containers as needed. When you have cleaned and prepared your game bird for freezing, wrap it in plastic, place it into an empty, 2-liter soda container. Cut away and remove the top of the container, fill 2/3 full with fresh clean water, (allow room for water expansion during freezing) and sit up right in your freezer and allow 48 hours to freeze rock hard. Not only will this ensure that your game birds remain fresh, but it allows you to stack them quite neatly in your freezer!

When asked what is considered the best of game birds to serve, my personal choice is the woodcock, pheasant, and quail. These birds have the finest of flavors, and are considered by the most avid of game bird hunters as the true picks of the litter. I will be publishing an entire cookbook dedicated to game birds and water fowl. I am sure you will enjoy the recipes contained in that cookbook! As for waterfowl, I must admit that that there is a not a goose or duck that I have cooked, that I have not liked. When it comes to waterfowl, I am a bit of a traditionalist. I tend to prepare them using "older, traditional recipes" at home. I believe that the flavors of a fine plump goose or duck should be savored, and remain uncluttered. Of course, those are my tastes. I encourage you to take your game to what ever limit or realm your heart desires!

Fish is normally cut into fillets, steaks, or retained whole. I tend to prepare and clean my smaller game fish, such as trout, and freeze them whole. Larger fish such as catfish, pike or salmon, I tend to trim and cut them into either fillets or steaks. I have few recommendations for fish other then fish, must remain as fresh as possible until you can prepare them for freezing. I will recommend that fish, should also be frozen, in small blocks of ice. This will preserve your fish and allow the best, long term storage results. Follow the same procedures as for freezing ducks, and game birds.

EQUIPMENT, TOOLS, AND DEFINITIONS

I felt compelled to add this brief chapter to simplify any questions that arise pertaining to the need for any special equipment for the preparation, cooking, and serving of a game gourmet meal. I shall present this chapter with a "chef's eye view" of kitchens, and would like to pass on a few words of experience to those budding home chefs amongst you.

The golden rule of professional kitchens is you have the tools and equipment necessary to perform your duties and tasks. All other items of equipment, although nice to have, tend to become more of an expensive hindrance, then a helper. If you had the opportunity to visit a professional kitchen, you would soon realize that to produce food on a daily basis, a kitchen depends on nothing more then a few basic items. Good quality knives, assorted pots, pans, baking sheet pans, ovens and ranges. There may be a need for a few specialized hand tools, or pieces of equipment. By, and large, most professional kitchens produce meals daily with a very basic and functional, amount of equipment.

Therefore, to prepare gourmet game meals at home will require you to purchase nothing. I will recommend to you a few basic items that are common in most households that frequently cook and prepare foods, and provide to you some basic information on why I prefer to use certain items in my kitchen.

Large equipment is not required to prepare large wild game, or any dish. I maintain a well-equipped and well-provisioned kitchen by virtue of my profession. The following "large equipment items" are what I regularly use to prepare foods on a daily basis.

1. Counter Top Mixer. I use this item for every conceivable dish and it has become a fine addition to my kitchen. I invested in a Kitchen Aid unit, due to the amount of food that I produce and experiment. Any small 1 quart, counter top mixer will suffice.
2. Food Processor. I own a professional-grade food processor, but use a $59.00 food processor on a daily basis. Do not invest in a food processor, unless you plan to use it. Do not pay "big bucks" for a state of the art system. Shop around, and find a less expensive unit that is tough, works and fits your needs.
3. Coffee Grinder. I use this little workhorse for preparing all of my seasoning blends. It is cheap, (under $20.00) and it works better then most food processors.
4. Blender. I own several blenders. The most commonly used blender is an off the shelf model that cost under $30.00 dollars. It works well for any household production needs, and will work well for any recipe in this cookbook.

These are the large items that I use on a regular and consistent basis.

Small tools and hand knives are the next items that are essential in my kitchen. I have many different types of small "toys and play things" that I have acquired during my years in the food business. To be honest, 98% of these tools are either placed away, or are used once a year for a special project. My recommendations for tools are as follows.

1. French Knife or Chefs Knife. I recommend that you invest in a good pair of French Knives. Stay away from the $2.00 on sale specials. They are cheap, and are a pain to keep sharpened. An 8 inch and 10 inch French will allow you the versatility to perform any task in a kitchen. A French knife is used for everything from chopping, to slicing and dicing.

2. Utility Knife. A utility knife is six to eight inches long, and is primarily used for cutting fruits, vegetables and salads. It can also perform double duty as a slicer for goose, duck and game birds.

3. Paring Knife. A must have in your kitchen. Between 2 to 4 inches in length, this versatile knife can be used for trimming, paring fruits and vegetables, and for garnish work.

4. Fillet or Boning knife. This knife usually has a 6 inch blade, and is designed to bone and fillet meats, fish, and fowl. I recommend two of these knives. One with a heavy blade for meat and fowl, and a flexible, lighter blade for fish.

5. Carving or Slicing Knife. This long bladed knife is used to produce fine carving cuts. It allows you to thin slice large cuts of meats.

6. Bread Knife. A long bladed, serrated, 8 to 10 inches in length knife used to slice breads, cakes, and baked items.

7. Butcher's Knife. I would recommend that you have one good butcher's knife for trimming, cutting and working with large pieces of meat. Keep this knife sharp, and well edged.

8. Vegetable Peeler. I buy a new peeler about every six months. I tend to use my paring knife for peeling items more then most folks. I do not like a dull peeler, so I change them out frequently. It is essential for peeling vegetables, and as a garnishing tool.

9. Meat Fork or Cook's Fork. A two tined, large fork used in carving meats, lifting hot pieces of meat and as a stabilizer in cutting and trimming birds and meats.

10. A small assortment of metal and rubber spatulas, slotted solid and perforated spoons. A skimmer, (used for skimming soups and stocks,) several pair of metal tongs, several whisks, (both heavy and light) a small Zester, a few ladles, in measured amounts, a box grater, several brushes, (for pastry and basting) a colander, and a china cap or Chinois for straining soups, sauces and stocks.

11. Cutting Boards and Grips. I would recommend that you have several cutting boards, with one designated for meats, one for fowl and fish, and one exclusively for fruits and vegetables. This separation of cutting boards prevents the possibility of bacterial cross-contamination. Always use a grip to prevent your cutting boards from slipping. It will save your fingers!

12. Thermometers. This is the first line of defense in any kitchen to prevent food poisoning, due to undercooked foods. I can not emphasize the importance of cooking foods to a proper and safe temperature. I have several thermometers, one for high temperatures, and one that temps foods up to 220 degrees. It is essential when cooking any meat, fowl or fish (either wild game or domesticated meats) that you cook your foods to a safe temperature!

13. Mixing Bowls and Measuring Cups and Spoons. I would have one good set of each. I have met folks that have more forms of measuring devices then can be counted. Trust me. One good set of each is all that is necessary.

A basic assortment of pots and pans are necessary to prepare and cook any type of meal. Here are a few recommendations as to what you should have, and what pots and pans work best.

1. Stock Pots. Two, three to five gallon stockpots are recommended in the production of stews, stocks, and for simmering large amounts of liquids.

2. Sauce Pans. Several saucepans ranging from one to six quarts should satisfy any cooking needs that you have. These pans are used for sauces, soups, vegetables, and general cooking.

3. Straight-sided Sauté Pans. This pan resembles a saucepan, except it is heavier, with shorter sides. It is used for sautéing, frying, preparing sauces, and browning meats. I use this pan on a daily basis, and have come to depend on this versatile cooking pan.

4. Slant sided Sauté Pan. This is commonly referred to as a fry pan, or skillet. This pan is used for general frying, sautéing, and cooking of meats, vegetables or eggs. I do not use coated or "stick proof" pans except for eggs. The sloped sides of this pan allow you to flip or turn your foods.

5. Cast Iron Skillet. I would recommend that you have both a large and small cast iron skillet. Cast iron is best used for roux production, and frying, as to the even heat distribution that cast iron allows.

6. Assorted Baking Sheets, several Bake Pans, (for larger meats, fowl or fish) and several large roasting pans, both with and without covers.

A brief bit of information for you about why proper pots and pans are necessary for good cooking results. Good pots and pans should be able to distribute heat evenly across the surface of the cooking pan. You do not want a pan that has "hot spots", as it will allow your foods to burn or scorch. The thickness of the metal and the composition of the metal are the predominant factors as to how well a pot or pan will allow you to cook. I personally use restaurant grade pots and pans at home. They are less expensive then the "pretty, fancy" cook sets that you see in most stores, and they are designed to withstand a beating, and abuse. If you look in the phone book under "New and Used Restaurant Supply", you can equip your kitchen with superior products, that will last a life time, for half the cost of store bought, retail pots and pans.

What types of metals or materials work best in a kitchen? My first choice is Aluminum cookware. It is lightweight, durable, and conducts heat evenly over the cooking surfacc. Aluminum does not react well to strong, acidic foods, and may discolor some foods if a wire or metal whisk or spoon is used. By far, commercial grade cookware is the best!

Cast Iron is my next favorite choice of cookware. It provides the best degree of heat distribution; it is heavy and allows you to fine-tune your cooking and frying. I love old, classic cast iron ware, and actually collect vintage cast iron!

Copperware is a great heat conductor, but is very expensive, and must be lined to prevent adverse chemical reactions and toxic reactions while cooking. Copper ware is usually lined with stainless steel, and requires a lot of polishing and up-keep.

Stainless steel ware is a poor heat conductor, and tends to be fancy and expensive, but for cooking, I do not own a single piece of stainless cookware.

Enamel ware, or Porcelain lined pots and pans should not be used. They are outlawed in most if not all commercial kitchens, and are outlawed in many areas by the health department. These pans chip and scratch very easily, which can allow bacteria to hide and thrive, and there are certain types of "gray enamel" that can be toxic if chipped!

Glass ware, stone ware or earthenware, has a limited use, in that they do not react to acidic foods, and do allow you to slow cook some types of food. The drawbacks to these products are they tend to be poor heat conductors, and tend to overcook your foods unless attention and care are used during cooking. The greatest liability to this cookware is that it will easily chip or break if not handled correctly.

I do not expect you or require you to run out and invest a grand amount of money on new cookware or equipment. I have cooked professionally for years with what I have listed. Most kitchen equipment is superfluous, and is a waste of money. If you watch a cooking show on cable, or on your local station, observe what the "professionals" use to prepare their meals. Do not be taken in by every new gadget that pops up on the market. I would hate to estimate home many closets are stuffed full of salad shooters and magic slicers! Stick to the basics. These items work, and that is what any cook, chef or home gourmet needs.

THE ART OF THE MARINADE

Two of the more frequently asked questions that have crossed my desk is by both novice hunters, and cookers of wild game are "What is a soak or marinade and why do you marinade the game?" There are several reasons. First, when you shoot game, a chemical reaction takes place in the animal's body. There is, for no better description, a " rush of adrenaline", that causes the animal's muscles to "grab" or tighten. By using a marinade, or "wild game soak", or "game draw", you are chemically causing the muscle and the muscle fiber to yield, or loosen, and cast off some of those unwanted bodily chemicals. Without soaking or marinating, you will have a "gamier flavor, and this is the primary reason you soak fresh, wild game. Remember to take into account what type of game you are taking, what type of vegetation they fed on, whether it was a lean year, etc. All game has both a unique and ingrained flavor common to their spices. Game flavors and tenderness is, in many cases dictated by environment, diet, and type of game.

Secondly, marinating acts as a tenderizing process. Using varied combinations of wines, oils, seasonings, spices and vegetables, you exchange and embed flavors and enhance the overall tenderness of the meat. By using a vast number of spice blends, seasonings, dry rubs, liquid marinades and soaks, I have been able to tenderize or soften game meat to a more desirable stage of tenderness and flavor. The object is not to detract or remove the flavor that makes game dishes unique. The goal is to soften what is not. To make tender, what is not. How you cook your game also plays pivotal role in the final out come of the dish. If you want venison to taste like beef, and have the exact same texture as beef, then simplify the hunt and shoot a cow! For, rattlesnake does not taste like chicken! It tastes like rattlesnake. Venison is venison, elk is elk, and bear is bear. There will always be a hint, or under lying taste of that game animal, but that is what makes it truly natures gourmet gift to the pallet! We are blessed to have a broad variety of wild game to choose from, which allows us, as sportsmen and women a virtual gourmet's table to prepare, taste and sample!

Third, by marinating, you take the meat in a direction that you want. If you have a particular taste that you wish to exploit, then by adding the desired spices or liquids to the soak, you can achieve a flavor that is both different and satisfying to your pallet! Never be afraid to play with your tastes, or to experiment. Some of the best recipes and game dishes that I have ever tried, would make a West Coast, high dollar eatery, weep with jealously, the recipes came from some "Good Ol' Boy", cooking in his doublewide, in East Texas. Have fun! Enjoy! Get Hot! Get Wild!

Finally, there are a few basic points to remember about Soaks and Marinades. Most cookbooks neglect to mention these simple facts they are very often over looked by most individuals, except, and including some chefs. First, marinades and soaks have a finite usage life. There is no reason why a properly prepared and stored soak or marinade cannot be re-used, several times. Depending on the ingredients, some marinades may be prepared weeks ahead, thereby, providing a deeper, richer flavoring to the meat. Each time you use your marinade, you reduce the concentration of flavors and seasonings, which will effect the desired results. You may have to boost the seasonings in order to regain the desired flavor. Also, please, remember that you are working with raw meats and fish. Use common sense when preparing and handling raw game meats and fish. The traditional technique of soaking or marinating was to place the meats in the soak at room temperature for a few hours. What folks did not realize was that although it did seem to work well at removing the gamy flavor, inadvertently, they had also created a little "bacteria factory". That is why refrigeration is critically important! You must also be aware, that blood and other fluids will leach out of the meat and into the marinade during the soaking process. This not only dilutes the flavor of the soak, but also can present a nasty health hazard if not properly stored, and reused no more then three times. Never use a soak or marinade with other game. You do not want to cross-contaminate your meats. An example would be using a soak for duck, then for venison. If you prepare a marinade or soak, I recommend that you always pour the liquid over the game, and if there is a portion remaining, store for reuse. Do not add used soaks or marinades to unused marinades. Always cover when storing, as to prevent contamination of your marinades. Soaks and Marinades have a very limited shelf life. Mark and date the mixture to prevent using an old product. My rule of thumb is "When in doubt – throw it out!"

BASIC SEASONED BUTTERMILK SOAK (This marinade, recommended for younger, tender game or for purchased game cuts)

Ingredients:
1 Quart Buttermilk
1 Tablespoon Black Ground Pepper
1 Tablespoon Salt
1 Tablespoon Garlic Powder
1 Tablespoon Onion Powder

Preparation: Place ingredients into bowl and whisk together for about 1 minute. Place your cleaned and rinsed cut of game, (venison, elk, and antelope) into a soaking container that will allow you to cover the meat with the soak or marinade. Pour soak over meat, (being sure that the meat is covered), cover or wrap the container, and place in the refrigerator for no less the 6 hours, 24 hours for best results. When ready to cook, remove from soak, and discard the remainder of the soak. Never use soaks or marinades to prepare a sauce!

TART VINEGAR SOAK/MARINADE

(This soak is best for older, gamier meat. This will pull the "gamier" flavors down a lot, but you may also have to resort to a tenderizer to soften the meat up.)

Ingredients:
4 Cups distilled Water (or filtered water)
1 Cup Cider Vinegar
1 Cup Red Wine
1 Tablespoon Lemon Juice
1 Teaspoon Salt
1 Teaspoon Black Pepper
½ Cup Oil

Preparation: Mix ingredients together in a bowl and whisk together with 1 quart of the distilled or filtered water. Pour remaining water into mixing bowl until you have 1 gallon of soak. Place smaller cuts into plastic bags or larger cuts of game into a clean, rinsed trash bag. Add the soak mixture, and store in your refrigerator for 24 hours. Remove meat, and discard soak. Rinse meat, and prepare to cook. Never use soaks or marinades to prepare a sauce!

SOUTHERN STYLE "RED NECK" GAME MARINADE

This marinade, was given to me, by a good friend from Alabama, who was a chef. His "Gran-daddy" taught him this soak, and prepared by his family for "takin care of game."

Ingredients:
1 Quart of water
3 to 4 Cans Beer
1 Tablespoon of Black Pepper
½ Tablespoon of Salt
½ Pound of Smoked Bacon
¼ Cup of Liquid Smoke
½ Cup Oil (Regular or Peanut Oil)
½ Cup Brown Sugar

1 (20oz) Bottle of Dr. Pepper

Preparation: Chop bacon and sauté until bacon is lightly cooked. Remove from heat, and hold, but do not let the grease harden. In a bowl, add water, beer, brown sugar, oil, salt, pepper, Liquid Smoke & bacon, with the drippings, whisk all ingredients together, and pour over your game. Allow the meat to soak for 48 hours. This is a great marinade if your are getting your game ready to smoke or Bar-B-Que! Discard marinade after use.

CHILI PEPPER TEXAS MARINADE

If you like things a little HOTER & WILDER like I do, then here is a game marinade/soak to light your fire!

Ingredients:
1 Cup finely diced onion
1 Cup coarsely cut green onions
1 16 oz Bottle of catsup
6 oz of Spicy Brown Mustard
½ cup of vinegar
1 tablespoon of chili powder
1/3 cup of minced garlic
1 Tablespoon of Tabasco or hot sauce
1 Tablespoon of salt
1 Cup of Lemon juice
1/3 Cup chopped Jalapeno Peppers with juice
1 6 0z bottle of Worchester sauce
1 cup butter

Preparation: Sauté onions, garlic, Jalapeno Peppers in butter, slowly for about 20 to 30 minutes, until soft and tender. In a large pan or pot, combine ½ gallon of water, 1 cup of white wine, and the rest of the ingredients. Heat, until liquid is steaming, but do not boil.

When liquid is hot, add the Sautéed mixture, and simmer for about 30 minutes. Allow mixture to cool down to room temperature, and pour over meat and place in refrigerator, covered, for 12 to 24 hour.

TANGY CITRUS MARINADE

This is a great, all around marinade for game birds when you are grilling, searing or Bar-B-Que-ing!

Ingredients:
- 2 Cups of water
- 2 Cups of Orange Juice
- 1 Cup of Lemon Juice
- 1 Cup of Lime Juice
- 1 Cup of Pineapple Juice
- ½ Tablespoon of Ground Black Pepper
- 1/3 Tablespoon salt
- ½ Tablespoon of Garlic Powder
- ½ Tablespoon of Onion Powder
- 1 Tablespoon of Ginger (powdered)
- 1 Cup of White Wine
- ½ Cup Cooking Oil

Preparation: Combine all ingredients in a bowl and whisk vigorously for 1 to 2 minutes. Place game in a dish, and pour contents over meat. If for game birds, about 2-3 hours. For meat, about 12 hours.

BASIC BURGANDY RED MARINADE

(This is as basic as you can get! Good for all meats, including domestic.)

Ingredients:
- 4 Cups Water
- 3 Cups Burgundy Wine
- 1 8oz Can of Beef Broth
- 1 Tablespoon Fresh Ground Black Pepper
- ½ Teaspoon of Kosher Salt

½ Cup of oil

Preparation: In a small stock pot, add 4 cups of water, oil, wine, beef broth, salt and pepper. Bring to a boil and reduce by 1/3. Boiling down, or reducing the liquid, concentrates the flavor. Allow the reduced liquid to cool, then pour over the game, and allowing meat to soak, for 12 to 24 hours in your refrigerator. Before cooking, drain the meat and discard the marinade

BASIC WHITE WINE MARINADE

(This marinade is good for game fowl, small game. It can also be used for very young, larger game.)

Ingredients: 2 Cups White wine
4 Cups Water
1 8oz Can of Chicken Broth or Stock (Vegetable Broth may also be substituted)
1/3 Cup of Cooking Oil,
(Olive Oil, seasoned cooking oil may be used)
1 Teaspoon Parsley
1 Teaspoon Fresh Cracked Black Pepper
1 Teaspoon Kosher Salt

Preparation: In a small stock pot, combine 4 cups water, 2 cups white wine, chicken or vegetable broth or stock, pepper and salt, and parsley. Bring to a boil, and reduce by 1/3. Boiling down, or reducing, concentrates the flavors. Allow the reduced liquid to cool, then pour over the meat. Allow game birds to soak for 3 to 6 hours, and fish no more then 3 hours. Cover and place in you refrigerator. Before cooking, drain the marinade, and discard.

SWEET MILK MARINADE FOR VENISON

(Most hunters recommend soaking their game in milk. This is the time- honored method to "draw out the gamy flavor". Over the years, the quality and content of milk has changed. When grand-pa use to soak his game in milk, milk had a much higher fat & cream content then today's milks. Here is a remedy to that problem. It's called "sweetening the milk".)

Ingredients: 2 Cups ½ & ½, or 1 pint of Heavy Cream
3 Cups of Whole Milk
1 Tablespoon Freshly Ground Black Pepper
1 6oz Can of Evaporated Milk

Preparation: Combine whole milk, evaporated milk, ½ & ½, or heavy cream, pepper in a mixing bowl and whisk together for 1 minute. Pour contents of bowl over meat, cover, and place in refrigerator for 12 to 24 hours. Remove and discard soak before cooking.
(NOTE: This is far from fat free, but the fat is free! It will also give your game a wonderful, rich flavor, and soften up the toughest cuts of meat.)

SIPPIN WHISKEY MARINADE

I have known more then a few chef's (yours truly, included) that not only enjoy the virtues and merits of a good "sipping" whiskey, but also what a grand flavor it can add to meats. So to honor to all those good folks who enjoy this most pleasurable of taste combinations, try this recipe!

Ingredients: 2 Cups water
2 Cups Jack Daniel's Bourbon Whiskey
2 Cups Dark Beer
1 Cup Cooking Oil
1 Teaspoon salt
1 Teaspoon Fresh Ground Black Pepper

1 Teaspoon Garlic Powder
½ Teaspoon Onion Powder
1 Diced onion (diced or chopped finely)
¼ teaspoon Paprika

Preparation: Mix all ingredients in a bowl and whisk together for about 1-2 minutes. The oil will separate, so you will want to rub the meat with a bit of oil, before pouring the marinade over the meat. Place meat in an airtight container, (a snap tight container is best). Pour contents of bowl over the meat, seal the container, shake for 1-2 minutes to ensure that the meat is well saturated, and place into your refrigerator for 3 to 4 days. (I have some folks tell me that they have left the meat in the refrigerator for as long as to two weeks!) Remove container and shake vigorously, or turn the meat about ever six hours. After three days, remove the meat, and for best results slow grill with a "Bourbon Mop" comprised of the same ingredients as in the marinade, but by adding 1 bottle of your favorite Bar-B-Que sauce, or seasoned glaze. This is one of my personal favorites!

LEMON & LIME MARINADE FOR FISH

This is a relative, basic marinade for game fish. I have used it for salmon, trout, as well as for catfish and bass. I prefer to get "hotter end wilder" by adding chili oil, chili powder and a dash of red and green peppers to the marinade!)

Ingredients: 1 Cup Cooking Oil (olive oil for a richer taste)
¼ Cup Lime Juice
¼ Cup Lemon Juice
¼ Cup Wine Vinegar
¼ Cup finely chopped Green Onions (both tops and bottoms)

2 Tablespoons of Fresh Cracked Black Pepper
½ Teaspoon of Kosher Salt

Preparation: Place all ingredients into a bowl and whisk for 1 to 2 minutes. Place fish into a pan, pour contents of bowl over fish, coating completely. Then turn fish several times to ensure an even coating. Cover and place in your refrigerator for 2 to 4 hours.
Before baking or broiling, add a few thin slices of lime and lemon, a little black pepper, and a teaspoon of fresh dill for that extra bit of flavor!

HOT & WILD CHILI & SOY MARINADE FOR FISH

For those who like that taste of the Orient, especially for fish, this marinade is hoot! Not only does this combine that Far-Eastern flavor, but allows the fish to bite back!

Ingredients:
½ Cup of Soy Sauce
½ Cup of Dry White (Sweet) Wine
1 Tablespoon of Sesame Oil
1 Tablespoon of Oriental Hot Chili Oil
1 Tablespoon of finely minced garlic
1 Teaspoon of Ginger
½ Teaspoon of Oriental or Hot Chinese Mustard
1 Teaspoon of Fresh Lemon Juice
1 Cup finely chopped Green Onions

Preparation: Combine all ingredients, place a bowl, and whisk together for 1-2 minutes. Place fish in a pan, and pour marinade over fish, coating evenly. Turn fish several times and evenly coat both sides of the fish to ensure good and equal absorption, cover, and place in refrigerator. Allow fish to marinade for 30 – 45 minutes. If the fish has a high fat content, (such as salmon) allow fish to marinade for 1 hour to 1 ½ hours. I personally prefer to grill when using this marinade. Grilled Oriental Vegetables, steamed rice, and a spicy honey mustard sauce make for some great eating! Its heart healthy too!

MARINADE FOR LARGE GAME

If there is an all around large game marinade, then this is a good one. It is uncooked, allowing all the flavors of the raw vegetables and spices to combine. It is flavorful, rich and bold. A fellow chef who hunts in the North-East suggested this recipe, as it has been kicking around for a number of years. When he prepares a venison dish, this is the soak, marinade that he uses to season & soften his game meat.

Ingredients:
- 2 Large, Whole Yellow Onions, Sliced
- 3 Carrots, Peeled, Sliced
- 3 Stalks Celery, with the tops, Chopped
- 1 Tablespoon Fresh chopped Parsley
- 2 Bay Leaves
- ½ Tablespoon Thyme
- 1 Tablespoon Rosemary
- 1 Teaspoon of Kosher Salt
- 1 Tablespoon Fresh Ground Black Pepper
- ¼ Teaspoon Ground Cloves
- 4 Cups of Claret, or a hardy, Burgundy Wine
- 1 Cup Wine Vinegar
- 1 Cup Extra Virgin Olive Oil
- 1 Cup of Apple Cider

Preparation: Combine all ingredients in a large mixing bowl; whisk together for 2 – 3 minutes. Cover the bowl, and let stand for 2-3 hours to allow time for the ingredients to blend before the meat, is added to the marinade. Place meat in a large container, pour marinade over meat, cover and place in your refrigerator for 48 to 72 hours. Remember to turn the meat every 6 to 8 hours to ensure proper absorption by the meat. This marinade will work well on large cuts of meat, or roasts. This recipe will marinade 10 to 15 pounds of game a one time.

Chef CY Young's hints for Soaks and Marinades

1. Select Fresh ingredients for preparing your soaks or Marinades.
2. Prepare the ingredients to be marinated ahead of time. Have the meat, fish or bird, cleaned, de-boned, trimmed of excess fat and gristle. Place in the pan or container you in which you wish to marinate.
3. Prepare the components for the marinade or the marinade itself ahead of time.
4. Adding the marinade, remember to cover the meat completely and evenly, turning several times, and then turning the meat as the recipe instructs.
5. Soak or marinate the meat for the length of time that the recipe instructs the type of meat, or to achieve the desired results when cooking.
6. Have fun and enjoy!
7. Never combine old marinades or soaks with fresh ones.

RUBING GAME THE RIGHT WAY: DRY RUBS

There are two types of marinades. There are liquid marinades, and there are dry marinades, commonly referred to as "Dry Rubs". Rubs achieve, (to a lesser degree) the same purpose as liquid marinades. They flavor the meat by using a specific combination of spices and herbs which, when combined produce a desired flavor. Rubs also aid in tenderizing cuts of meat, and game birds but not as well as a liquid.

First, there is needed, a bit of clarification between the terms seasoning, herbs, and spices. Spices are usually produced from seeds, roots, berries, barks, or in the example of salt, a mineral, either mined, or produced from the dehydration of seawater. Fruits are also used in producing some spices. Herbs are produced from a diverse array of flowers and leaves. There is also a third category, known as the "aromatics". These pungent vegetables are more familiar to us as garlic, shallots, etc. Seasoning therefore can be simply deduced as the combination of individual spices, which results in a particular flavor. Herbs may be added to the spices to enhance and further impact a certain flavor or taste. Some herbs are subtle. They can add a background flavor to a dish, or when allowed to marinade with a meat to enhance the flavor. Other herbs are best added at the final stage of cooking, or as the dish is served which when combined add their own unique impact on both the dish, as well as the pallet.

.

I have had friends describe a favorite home recipe and explain that they seasoned the chicken with fresh basil, rosemary and butter. My response was that they in fact had produced an herb rub for the dish. Their answer was, "No I seasoned it!" There is a difference between the two. Think of good old Col.

Sanders, with his secret blend of herbs and spices! Even the Col. knew the difference!

I have taken the time to explain and define these differences for a reason. When preparing a recipe for dry rub, or dry marinade, such as those recipes presented in this chapter, you may have a clearer understanding as to any subtle phrasing, and will eliminate any possible confusion. If I refer to seasoning a particular dish, and then refer to an herbal rub, please do not add the seasonings again, to the herbs, there by over seasoning the dish. I am sure that I have confused you to the point of stomping puppies. I have also provided some of you with 15 minutes of dinner conversation that will enthrall, if not amaze your friends or relatives at your next dinner party!

The term "Dry Rub", is also deceptive. Most of the ingredients that you will commonly use, purchase or have on hand are in fact, dry. Most herbs that you will use to prepare game rubs will be dehydrated and finely chopped. If you wish to invest in fresh herbs, it is money well spent. If you have the where with all to produce your own small garden of fresh herbs, then, (by all means), do so. You will gain an ample and diverse supply of fresh herbs to cook with and enjoy. It will allow you to add a considerable depth of taste to foods you prepare and cook. The remainder of the populace, both amateur, and professional alike will be consigned to what we can find in our local grocery isle!

In most cases, you will first, rub, or massage the meat, fish, or bird with a very light coat of oil, flavored oil, olive oil, melted butter, or liquid. Fish, are usually soaked in water before preparation, but do not let the wetness of the meat deceive you. I would advise you to use an oil or butter, as you would any other meat. This light coating of oil or liquid will assist in the cooking process whether you are searing, grilling or baking the meat. More important, a light coating of oil or butter will provides a medium for the spices and herbs to adhere too. In some recipes, you will create a damp rub, or paste, to work into the game that you are preparing to cook. In addition, using olive oil, or seasoned oils, will add a desired flavor to the game. Oils and butters are part of the recipe, and they are included for a reason. Butter adds taste because it contains fat. That is why gourmets will use only butter for certain recipes. If you have ever ordered a lean cut of meat at a restaurant, and it arrives at you table with a slice of compound butter on top, you know why. That butter and herb blend are there to activate and compliment the taste of the meat, fowl or fish. In fine cooking, butter is our friend!

Finally, dry marinades, or dry rubs, traditionally, remain on the meats or fish you intend to cook. You do not have to purge, drain, shake or rinse away this marinade. Dry marinades require less preparation time, may be produces in large or small batches, and have a shelf life longer then your average Egyptian mummy. Importantly, it allows you, the novice home chef, to develop and build on some of the basic recipes that are on these next few pages. Have fun! Class, you are, dismissed!

A Helpful Tip from the Chef, for Beginners: The Less is More Principle.

When learning the art of seasoning or preparing herbed dishes, remember that less is more! When dealing with wild game, you do not to bury the entire flavor of the game with too much seasoning and herbs. Your should give life, and enhance the flavor of the meat or fowl, not bury it. “Seasonings and herbs should be an art of the sublime”, a chef once told me. “You should tread lightly when spicing a dish, verses marching down a too well seasoned path.” Less is more! Rather “sage” advice, don’t you think?

QUICK & SIMPLE DRY RUB

This recipe was given to me (years ago), by a great Bar-B-Q'er in Austin, Texas. He said that the trick was in the rub, and in the slow smoking time. It did not matter what you were cooking, the rub had to be smooth, and "worked in real good". This rub is excellent for and large game destined for the smoker, Bar-B-Que or grill.

Ingredients:
- ¼ Cup Cracked Black Pepper
- 1 Tablespoon Kosher Salt
- 1 Tablespoon Garlic Powder
- 1 Tablespoon Onion Powder
- ¼ Tablespoon Paprika
- ¼ Teaspoon Chili Powder

Preparation: Soak game meat in a bath or soak of ½ gallon of water, two cans of beer, and 1- 2 cups cider vinegar for 24 hours. Remove meat; allow to drain and place on a firm flat surface. The meat should be damp, but not wet. Combine all ingredients for rub in a small mixing bowl. Using a small whisk, blend spices evenly. Using a tablespoon portion of rub, evenly sprinkle it over the meat. If it is a large cut of meat, use two table spoon portions. Rub spice evenly and firmly into meat. You want an even coating, and to have the spice worked well into the meat. When completed, wrap meat in plastic wrap, or foil, place in refrigerator for 3 to 6 hours. Remove and cook as desired.
(NOTE) You may leave the meat to "season" for 24 hours if you so desire. It is up to you.

KICK BUTT SOUTH OF THE BOARDER RUB

This rub is not for the faint of heart or pallet. This damp rub has been named by some folks as the "Barn Burner". With the right sauce, (which is included in this book) you can fire up any cold fall or winter night! This will be a Damp Rub.

Ingredients: ¼ Cup Fresh Ground Black Pepper
1 Tablespoon Kosher Salt
1 Tablespoon Chili Powder
½ Teaspoon Cumin
¼ Teaspoon Cayenne Pepper
¼ Cup Finely Minced Garlic
2 Very Finely Minced Serrano Peppers
¼ Cup Finely Minced Sweet Onion
¼ Cup Finely Chopped Cilantro (Fresh)
2 Tablespoons of Mesquite Liquid Smoke
2 Liquid Ounces of Tequila
2 Tablespoons Lime Juice
¼ Cup Cooking Oil

Preparation: Soak game meat for 24 hours in a bath 1 quart of water, 1 Cup of Cider Vinegar, 1 Cup of Tequila. Remove game meat from bath. Place on wire rack and allow to drain, and pat dry with paper towels. Combine the Liquid Smoke, oil, tequila and lime juice, in a small bowel; whisk for 1 minute. Dip out about 2 to 3 tablespoons of liquid and rub deeply into the meat. Combine other ingredients into a bowl and mix together with a whisk, or wooden spoon. Remove 2 to 3 teaspoons of the damp rub and work it well into the meat. Wrap in plastic, place into your refrigerator for 3 to 6 hours. You want to allow this rub to combine and sweat into the meat. Remove, and (for best results) slow grill using my "Barn Burner Mop" included in this book.

FALL HARVEST APPLE AND PEAR DAMP RUB

I have always enjoyed the recipes of our forefathers. They were blessed in many ways with (although limited) fresh fruits and herbs that we now take for granted. Their recipes were simple. They used what they had in season, or what they were able to preserve or can. This recipe is a variation on an old recipe that I found many years ago, and it conjured up images of log homes, yeast baked breads, and fresh venison, roasting on a spit! This recipe for seasoned damp rub was designed for wild game roasts of 5 to 7 pounds. To be slow roasted, and the juices and drippings saved for "succulent gravy".

Ingredients:
- 1 Cup Bacon, Diced (Smoked bacon)
- 1 Cup Fresh Minced Shallots
- 3 Tablespoons Sherry Wine Vinegar
- 3 Tablespoons Red Wine or Claret
- 2 Teaspoons Dijon Mustard
- 1 Tablespoon Fresh Cracked Black Pepper
- 1 Teaspoon Kosher Salt
- 2 Teaspoons Thyme (Freshly Minced)
- 1 Teaspoon Fresh Rosemary
- ¼ Teaspoon Allspice
- 1 Fresh Pear (Pealed and finely diced)
- 1 Large Apple (Pealed, cored and Finely Diced)
- ¼ Cup Apple Cider
- ¼ Cup Pear Nectar
- 1 Cup Finely Minced Red Onion
- ¼ Cup Oil

Preparation: Soak your game roast for 24 hours in a bath of ½ gallon of water, 1 cup cider vinegar, 1 cup red wine, 2 cups of apple cider. Remove game, and place in roasting pan on a wire rack. Cut several small slits in the meat and insert a thick cut piece of seasoned bacon. This will add fat to aid in the cooking, and enhance the flavor greatly!

In a skillet, combine the bacon, shallots, red onion, red wine or claret, apple and pear, and slowly sauté on low heat. You want to slowly combine and meld these flavors together. When these ingredients are soft, (cooking on low heat for 30 minutes) remove the mixture from the skillet, and empty into a bowl and allow to cool. Yes, bacon drippings also! When your sauté has cooled, add all other ingredients and whisk together. Your rub should be thick with the consistency of syrup. Use a small measuring cup and scoop out a portion of the rub. Work the rub into the meat well, coating the entire roast. If you have any rub remaining, add 1 cup of red wine and use as to baste during cooking. You can save the drippings and at the conclusion of cooking use this as a base for an excellent fruit hunter sauce!

HUNTERS SPICE AND HERB DRY RUB (SEASONED SALT)

I am sure that all of you are great hunters and sportsman, and always return home with your limit of game each season. Therefore, I felt compelled to include a bulk recipe for a general spice and herb dry rub that, can be easily made, and stores well. Commonly referred to by many as Seasoned Salt, because the primary spice is salt! In reality it is an herbal spice blended salt. Hey! What's in a name!

Ingredients:

1 Cup Salt (If you prefer Kosher salt, the place in a food processor and grind until a fine granulated consistency. You will need to add extra Kosher salt, to equal 1 cup of fine salt.)
1 Tablespoon Corn Starch
2 Tablespoons Paprika
1 Teaspoon Mace
1 Teaspoon Cayenne Pepper
2 Teaspoons Ground Celery Seed
2 Tablespoons Black Pepper
2 Teaspoons Garlic Powder
3 Teaspoons Onion Powder
2 Teaspoons Curry Powder
2 Tablespoons Chili Powder
2 Teaspoons Oregano
1 Teaspoon Marjoram

1 Teaspoon Thyme
1 Teaspoon Rosemary
2 Tablespoons Dry Mustard
½ Tablespoon Dill

Preparation: Place all dried herbs into a food processor (or coffee grinder) and reduce to as fine a powder as possible. If there are small bits of coarse material remaining, pass through a fine sieve. Mix all remaining ingredients together, blending together with a fine whisk. Pour into a container or shaker, and use as desired.

TANGY SWEET MUSTARD DAMP RUB

This damp rub is very good on small game, and small game birds. It adds a nice flavor when well rubbed into the game and left for 24 hours before cooking. Please remember, if using on game birds, no matter what seasonings or herbs you use, they only go as far as the skin. If you wish too properly season any whole game bird, then you will need additional seasonings inside the body cavity.

Ingredients: 4 Tablespoons Dry Mustard
¼ Cup Sugar
¼ Cup Brown Sugar
1 Teaspoon Hot Chili Oil
¼ Cup Vinegar
2 Tablespoons Butter (Softened)
½ Teaspoon Kosher Salt
½ Teaspoon Fresh Cracked Black Pepper
¼ Cup Honey

Preparation: Soak game in a bath of 3 cups water, 1 cup white wine, 1 cup vinegar for 12 to 24 hours. Remove game.

Remove excess liquid and pat to damp dry. Place game into a baking dish or pan, lightly oiled. Place all ingredients into a mixing bowl and (using a hand mixer) mix until all ingredients are completely and evenly blended. Your rub should be thick. Rub on game, cover and place into refrigerator for 3 to 6 hours. Remove and cook.

CHIPOLTIE PEPPER DAMP RUB

This damp rub will enhance any venison, elk, boar, or antelope meat to an entirely new dimension. I would suggest using a food processor to create this rub. You want to create a paste, or pesto-consistency for this damp rub.

Ingredients:
- 1 Tablespoon Minced Garlic
- 3 Tablespoon Butter (Unsalted)
- 1/3 Cup Minced Green Onions (tops & bottoms)
- ¼ Cup Sun Dried Tomatoes (Re-hydrated & Chopped)
- 3 Large Chipotle Peppers (Remove stems and Seeds, Minced)
- ¼ Teaspoon Kosher Salt
- ¼ Teaspoon Fresh Cracked Black Pepper
- 2 Tablespoons Worcestershire Sauce
- ½ Cup Brown Sugar
- 1 Tablespoon Hot Sauce or Tabasco
- ¼ Cup Chopped Cilantro
- 2 Cups Chicken Broth

Preparation: Soak game in a bath of 3 cups of water, 1 cup red wine vinegar, and 1 cup of red wine. Allow game to soak for 12 to 24 hours. Remove meat, and pat to damp dry. Place on a flat pan, and prepare to rub. In a skillet, on low heat, melt butter. Add garlic, onions, sun-dried tomatoes, peppers, salt and pepper, Worcestershire sauce. Sauté slowly for 15 minutes.

Remove from heat and allow sauté mixture to cool for 10 minutes. Place all ingredients in food processor, including contents of skillet. Add ¼ cup of chicken broth to food processor, and begin to puree. Add broth slowly to mixture. You do not want to thin the rub too much.

When it reaches a consistency of a pesto, or pliable and smooth, then remove and rub deeply into game. If game is dry, then coat lightly with a mixture of 2 tablespoons of oil and 2 tablespoons of broth. Cover, and place in refrigerator for 12 to 24 hours. Remove and cook as desired. I personally prefer to either to lightly smoke or grill the meat.

DRY MARINADE FOR FISH

I have discovered that the key to a good recipe for fish is to be subtle with its base seasonings. I have always taught young cooks to go easy on the seasonings and herbs. The customer came here to eat fish, not a potpourri basket! If you prefer to taste the flavor of the fish, (especially Salmon and Trout) then this is a good, standard with which to season by.

Ingredients:
- 1 Tablespoon of Fresh Cracked Black Pepper
- 1 Teaspoon of Kosher Salt
- ¼ Teaspoon of Garlic Powder
- ¼ Teaspoon of Onion Powder
- 1 Tablespoon Finely Minced Fresh Chives
- 1 Tablespoon Finely Minced Parsley
- 2 Tablespoons of Fresh Lime Juice
- 1 Tablespoon of Fresh Lemon Juice
- 2 Cups of White Wine (Not too sweet or dry)
- 1/3 Cup Extra-Virgin Olive Oil

Preparation: Rinse and soak fish in ice water for 30 minutes. Remove fish and pat to damp dry. Place fish in pan and add wine, lime and lemon juice. Allow fish to soak for 3 hours. You have several options on how to prepare your catch. Refer to several of my recipes for ideas located in the Game Fish Gourmet Chapter of this book. Mix your spices together in a bowl, whisking for 1 minute. Brush a light coating of Olive Oil on the fish. Coat the fish evenly on both sides. Then sprinkle the seasoning evenly over the fish. Use fresh parsley and chives as a flavoring garnish when fish is ready to serve.

JERK DRY RUB SEASONING

While writing this book, a chef friend of mine suggested that I include one of his favorite rubs. He has used it to season game birds, and young, tender cuts of venison. I will leave the choice up to the reader. I prefer to use this rub on small game birds, such as quail, or young duck, and then slow roasted or smoked over a seasoned wood fire. If you prepare this dish with a game bird, then I suggest that you make fruit chutney, or a fresh fruit salsa to top this dish!

Ingredients:

1 Tablespoon Dried Chives
1 Tablespoon Onion Powder
1 ½ Teaspoon Chili Powder
1 Teaspoon Garlic Powder
1 Teaspoon Finely Milled Kosher Salt
¾ Teaspoon Brown Sugar
1 Teaspoon Fresh Cracked Black Pepper
½ Teaspoon Ground Ginger
½ Teaspoon Ground Coriander
½ Teaspoon Dried and Ground Thyme
½ Teaspoon Allspice
½ Teaspoon Ground Cinnamon
½ Teaspoon Dried Rosemary
½ Teaspoon Ground Cumin
½ Teaspoon Cayenne Pepper

Preparation: Place all spices and herbs into a mixing bowl and blend, together well. Take your selection of game, rinse, and pat dry. Rub game with a light coat of peanut oil, and rub jerk seasoning well into the meat. Cover and place into refrigerator for 3 to 6 hours. If you select venison or elk as your meat of choice, then marinade, in a mixture of 1 quart water, 1 cup spiced rum, 2 Tablespoons Lime Juice, 1 Tablespoons Lemon Juice, ¼ cup orange juice, and ½ Cup Brown sugar. Blend together, and soak meat for 12 to 24 hours, in refrigerator, covered. Remove, drain and then rub with Jerk Seasoning.

CARIBBEAN PASTE OR DAMP RUB

This rub has a blend of the Caribbean and Latin flavor. It will work well with most game. You must remember to marinade your large game in a marinade that will compliment this rub. I would use a mixture of spiced rum, and citrus flavors, as with the marinade for the jerk rub. I have also played with banana liqueur or mango nectar for a different twist. The important thing to remember is to tone down the game flavor, and tenderize the game before you season.

Ingredients:
- 1 Tablespoon Kosher Salt
- 1 Tablespoon Fresh Cracked Black Pepper
- ¼ Cup Finely Minced Onion
- 2 Tablespoons Minced Garlic
- 3 Tablespoons Brown Cane Sugar
- 1 & ½ Teaspoons Dried Chopped Thyme
- 1 & ½ Teaspoons Ground Cumin
- 1 & ½ Teaspoon Cumin
- 1 Teaspoon Paprika
- 1 Teaspoon Ground Cinnamon
- 1 Teaspoon Ground Clove
- 1 Teaspoon Cayenne Pepper

1 Beef Bullion Cube (dissolved in 2 Tablespoons Red Wine)
¼ Cup Peanut Oil

Preparation: Mix all seasonings and herbs in a small mixing bowl. The bullion cube should be soft, and can be pressed into a paste or crumbled in your hand. Using a whisk, blend in ½ teaspoon of oil with the seasoning and the bullion cube. You wish to create a soft paste mixture. Continue to add oil and mix until rub is smooth and fluid. Use remainder of oil to rub game, rub in seasoned rub, cover and place in refrigerator for 6 to 24 hours.

OLD LOUISIANNA STYLE DAMP RUB FOR FISH

In the South, especially in Louisiana, the art of seasoning fish and seafood is a perfected art form. When shellfish is prepared, a "boil" is added to the water or stock. This "boil" is what imbeds that grand and subtle flavor into the shellfish that produces that distinctive "Louisiana Flavor". It has made seafood and fresh caught dishes renowned. This is a damp rub variation for game fish, and may be used, for creating your own boil, if desired.

Ingredients:
½ Tablespoon Cayenne Pepper
1 Tablespoon Fresh Cracked Black Pepper
1 Tablespoon Crushed Red Pepper
2 Bay Leaves
½ Teaspoon Celery Seeds
½ Teaspoon Coriander
½ Teaspoon Ground Ginger
¼ Teaspoon Mace
½ Tablespoon Kosher Salt
1 Tablespoon Hot Sauce
1 Whole Lemon

Preparation: Combine all spices and herbs and place in a spice mill or coffee grinder. Grind until the seasoning is blended, and chopped finely. Remove any chafe from the seasoning mixture. Place in a small mixing bowl, and add hot sauce. Mix with a fork, and slowly add the lemon juice. Continue to mix until the seasoning has become a paste. Rub the fish with a light coating of white wine, and then rub in the seasoned damp rub. If you wish to create a "BOIL" using this recipe, cut the lemon into quarters, and add the spices, herbs and hot sauce whole, to 1 gallon of water. Bring to a boil, and add your shellfish. For a larger amount of seasoning, simply multiply this recipe for each gallon of water used.

SOUTHEAST ASIAN HOT & WILD DAMP RUB

This is a very common recipe throughout Southeast Asia that has a multitude of uses when cooking game. It is great with game bird, fish, and large game. If you want to cook a dish with a distinctive Southeast Asian taste, this is the recipe to use. This damp rub stores well in the refrigerator, and can be prepared weeks in advance. As it is a paste it may be added to rice to enhance its flavor, or with vegetables. A teaspoon will do when cooking. This is a very spicy rub. A small amount goes along way!

Ingredients:
- ½ Tablespoon Ground Coriander
- ½ Tablespoon Ground Cumin
- 1 Tablespoon Fresh Cracked Black Pepper
- ½ Cup Fresh Chopped Cilantro (Leaves Only)
- 1 Tablespoon Ground Ginger
- 2 Tablespoons Fresh Chopped Garlic
- 6 Fresh Green Onions, Finely Chopped
- 12 Fresh Serrano Peppers, (Stems and Seeds removed) coarsely chopped
- 1 Teaspoon Kosher Salt

1 Tablespoon Hot Chile Oil
1 Teaspoon Kosher Salt
1 Teaspoon of Vegetable Paste (Seafood or Shrimp Paste may be Substituted)
2 Tablespoons Fresh Lemon Juice
1 Teaspoon Lime Juice
¼ Cup Water

Preparation: Place Chili Oil, Lemon and Lime juice, paste, and water into a blender or food processor and blend for 30 seconds. Then add all remaining herbs and spices to the liquid until it becomes a paste. When you prepare this rub, blend on puree for best results.

LARGE GAME STIR FRY DAMP RUB

In a recent survey, out of three Americans eat some type of Chinese food at least once a week. I personally love to cook Chinese dishes with wild game. It has been a challenge to combine and blend these diverse flavors to achieve a balance that will, both complement the selected game, as well as the satisfy the pallet. One of my favorite recipes for large game is a pepper steak variation that when sautéed in a wok is great. I have included a garlic-ginger sauce recipe in this book that will complement this dish nicely.

Ingredients: 2 Tablespoons Minced Garlic
1 Tablespoon Ginger
½ Teaspoon Kosher Salt
2 Tablespoons Fresh Cracked Black Pepper
2 Teaspoons Sugar
4 Green Onions (Finely Chopped)
1 Medium Green Bell Peppers Finely Chopped
3 Tablespoons of Soy Sauce
2 Tablespoons of Teriyaki Sauce

3 Tablespoons of Peanut Oil

Preparation: Cut the desired large game meat (two – two and one half pounds) into 1 inch cubes. Place game into a large plastic bag or bowl and marinade in one cup of water, 1 cup rice wine vinegar, 2 tablespoons Teriyaki Sauce, 1 Teaspoon Soy Sauce, 1 Tablespoon Garlic Powder, and 1 Tablespoon Black Pepper. Cover or seal and refrigerate for 24 hours. Combine all other ingredients in a blender or food processor, and blend on puree. You want to create a paste. Drain any excess moisture from this rub. Three hours before cooking, remove meat from marinade, drain place meat into a large plastic bag, add the seasoned rub, and rub thoroughly rub into the meat. Refrigerate for 3 to 6 hours, and then cook.

STOCKS! THE RICHEST OF ALL TASTES

I have no clue as to why the vast majority of so called gourmet cookbooks that are marketed to the American public never venture into the most fundamental areas of cooking. The preparation and production of fresh stocks, for the home is the most simple of procedures and will add the highest of classical tastes to home gourmet cooking. I have dined at many friends' homes. They have spent many hours, and dollars buying only the best cuts of meat, freshest vegetables, and slaving to prepare a great dessert. When it came time to prepare a soup or sauce, they would reach into their pantry, and emerge with a little envelope of dry mix, or can of concentrate. They were about to commit the most common of culinary insults! Go ahead! Hang that Velvet Elvis on the wall of the Sistine Chapel while you are at it! Why take a great cut of fresh game meat, fish or game bird, and kill the flavor by pouring pre-packaged goop on top of it! It is beyond my understanding.

One of the first skills taught to me when I was learning the Chefs trade, was how to prepare a good stock. Stocks have always been a one of the most critical and important aspects of cooking and eating well. Stocks are the basis of all, great sauces, soups and stews. Stocks are used as a base element in vegetable dishes, in many main dishes that require stocks or "broth's" added for flavoring. To add to the dimension of a particular dish, a well-prepared stock is essential. "If a stock is not well prepared or is made in an imperfect manor," (I was told on many occasions), "your labors will be in vain". "The meal that you have prepared will be no better then fast food with secret sauce!"

As defined, a stock is simply a liquid, to which meats, fish, vegetables, herbs and seasonings are added, heated, simmered and reduced to produce a desired, concentrated flavor. Stocks are one of the easiest gourmet ingredients to prepare in a home setting. Stocks are slightly more labor intensive then some kitchen chores, but when mastered, fresh stocks will allow you to explore a galaxy of new tastes and cuisines. As a chef, I was always attempting to work into my budget, the purchasing of bones or meats for fresh stocks, and especially, game stocks. A fresh game stock is highly prized in gourmet kitchens, but costs are always a factor. Most kitchens use "out of the can" stocks and bases.

This is a cost saving measure in both labor, as well as production time. As a home gourmet cook, and sportsman you have the luxury of time, your own labor (let it be a labor of culinary love) and an outstanding source of fresh game.

There are three main stocks that you can produce at home, with nothing more then a large stock pot, cutting board, and knife. The seasonings are readily available at any local supermarket, and the process of rendering the stocks may be completed in a weekend. Once completed, the stocks can be frozen, allowing you to enjoy them through out the year, or until next hunting season.

The most basic of stocks are as follows: a white stock, a brown stock, and a vegetable stock. Fish stock falls into its own separate category, due to its limited uses. In the recipes that follow, stock preparation, and production are almost, step by step, the same. I have attempted to simplify the process, as well as the instructions to reduce any confusion. I have included a few "Chef's Helpful Hints" at the end of this chapter to give you, the budding at home, game gourmet, as much help as possible to both prepare, use and store your game stocks. I could produce an entirely separate book on sauces, soups, and uses for this wonderful bounty that most hunters simply discard as waste and trimmings. You shall have to wait just a short time for my forth book, which is dedicated to game sauces, soups and stews and other great things! Got ya!!!

STOCK PREPARATION: BASIC STEPS, TECHNIQUES AND TOOLS

As gourmet cooking goes, stocks are simple to produce. Stock ingredients are also simplistic in there composition. Patience and care are the key to producing a fine stock. There are several basic rules that must be followed when producing a stock. The first rule is to start with cold water, or liquid. Cold water or liquids will allow the flavors to be released into the water surrounding them, whether it is game birds, venison, elk, etc. The exception is when you brown the bones in the oven, which will produce a deeper, richer flavor then the cold immersion method. Simply stated, place your bones or meats into a stockpot with cold clear water, and allow to soak. The second step is known as clarification. A superior stock is "clarified" by removing as many small bits of fat and particles as possible. There are several skimming and sieving steps that will occur during the cooking process of your stock. Attention to detail, and care will produce a good clear stock. The third step is to skim carefully, and remove as much material as possible. Do not wash the bones or meat before you place it in the water, except to remove any questionable materials that may be on the meat or bones. The meat or bones should be "clean", but not washed. Step number four is very simply. Do not boil the stock! If you boil the stock to long, and if you use to high of heat, you will cloud the stock. It will be impossible to remove that cloudiness from that stock, and will make the end-result, less desirable. When I prepare stocks at home, I rent a couple of movies, break out the bourbon, and snuggle

with my wife! This does nothing to aid in the cooking process, but it makes a slow process a lot of fun!
Here are a few tips on simmering your stock. You want enough heat to create a slow role to the liquid. If there is too little heat, then the fats and other heavy materials will sink to the bottom of the pot. If these fats and materials sink to the bottom, they may burn, which will destroy the flavor of the stock. If the heat is too high, then the fats and scum will be impossible to skim. A trick that most chefs use is to "off-set" the stockpot on the heat source, not centered on the bottom of the pot. As your stock simmers, you will discover that most of the fats, and other nasty things will float to the surface early during the simmering process. This is when it is important to skim! I use a small ladle, and remove the fats and scum from around the sides of the pot. A fine mesh sieve is also desirable to remove that unwanted scum.

There is no set time when cooking a stock. It is a "by sight" cooking process. There are recommended times to add ingredients to the stock, and there are numerous debates as to when to add the vegetables and seasonings. The method that I am describing to you is the most standard way of stock production. I have taught my students and apprentices this method, as I was taught. It has worked for me, and has always produced fine results.

The next phase of stock production is adding the mirepoix, and the sachet. For most folks, this translates to the vegetables and seasonings. The vegetables consist of three items: carrots, onions and celery. The vegetables are chopped, and added to the stock, about ¼ of the way during the simmering process. The seasonings, or sachet, are added at this time. The seasonings are measured, placed in a small piece of cheesecloth, tied with a string, and placed into the pot to cook. I recommend that you cut a long enough piece of string so that one end may be tied to the "herb pouch" and the other can be tied to the handle of the stockpot. I like fishing, but hate the idea of fishing out a HOT seasoning bag!

When the stock is finished, you will drain and strain the liquid, removing all vegetables and bones from the stock. A small saucepan, a sieve, with cheesecloth works very well. The stock may be placed into small containers for the cooling process. DO NOT THROW AWAY THE BONES, OR VEGETABLES! These items can be reused to prepare a "remouillage", which means a "second wetting". The bones are placed into cold water, simmered again to produce a weaker stock. New meat and bones can be added to this liquid to begin the stock process all over again! My rule is that nothing should go to waste. America is blessed with the best selection of game for a sportsman to hunt or fish, so let us use wisely what the good lord has given us.

You are now ready to strain and cool your stocks. I recommend that you take a cone colander, line it with a piece of cheesecloth, and place it in an empty pot, in your sink. If you have two small bricks, or two small blocks of wood available, then place them into the sink first, and then sit your empty pot on them. This will allow your stock to cool equally from all sides. Fill the sink with ice and cold water to cool the stock, when it is "strained" into the empty pot. Bring the hot stockpot to the sink. Using a small saucepan, slowly dip the stock and strain the stock thru the colander. You may have to remove the cheesecloth and empty the contents of the colander several times to allow proper filtration of the stock. Remember to retain the bones and remaining vegetables for reuse, if you wish to prepare a remouillage. Allow the stock to cool, stirring occasionally to distribute the heat and aid with rapid cooling. When cool, you may package the stock for storage. I use several ice cube trays and freeze "stock cubes" for small amounts of stock. For larger amounts of stock, I measure out 1 quart of stock into a strong plastic bag or container, and place them into my freezer. These pre-measured amounts can be quickly thawed, and used through out the year.

What tools will you need to prepare these wonderful creations at home? The list is a short one. A good chef's knife, French knife, or small butcher's knife is recommended, for any cutting needs. Needed is a cutting board, a measuring cup, (a large 1 quart Pyrex measuring cup is best), a large stock pot, (5 gallons is good) a ladle or skimmer, a sieve, china cap or colander, cheese cloth, string and storage bags or containers. If you process your own large game, then you will need a small bone saw to cut down the larger bones. Congratulations! You now have the tools and are ready to produce all the game stocks you would want.

BASIC WHITE GAME STOCK

Ingredients: 10 – 12 Pounds of Bones (Game Bird, or Venison or Elk)
10 – 12 Quarts of Cold Water
(Items for the Vegetable Mirepoix)
1 Pound of Chopped Onion
8 oz of Chopped Carrot
8 oz of Chopped Celery
(Items for the Sachet, or the Herb Pouch)
1 Bay Leaf
¼ Teaspoon of Thyme
¼ Teaspoon of Whole Black Peppercorns
8 Fresh Parsley Stems
2 Whole Cloves

Special Items or Tools for Cooking: Cheesecloth, string

Preparation: If the venison or elk bones are whole, cut into 3 to 4 inch pieces, with a small meat saw. Rinse the bones lightly in cold water. If game bird bones, then rinse lightly and place into stockpot whole, without cutting. Blanch the bones by placing them into your stockpot, cover them with cold water, and bring them to a boil. When the blanching liquid has come to a full boil, remove form heat, drain and rinse the bones lightly. Place the bones back into the stock pot, add fresh cold water, bring back to a quick boil, reduce the heat and begin to simmer. Begin to skim the "scum" carefully. After skimming, add the vegetable mirepoix. Prepare the herb sachet by placing the herbs into the cheesecloth, and tie with string. Place the herb pouch into the stockpot. Simmer for 3 to 4 hours for game birds, 6 to 8 hours for venison or elk. You may need to add water to keep the bones covered. At the end of the cooking process, remove the stock from the heat, strain through the colander lined with several layers of cheesecloth, and allow stock to cool in a pot in an ice water bath. The stock is ready to refrigerate or freeze. This recipe will produce about 2 gallons of white game stock.

BASIC GAME BROWN STOCK

This recipe may be applied to most game, by substituting bones and trimmings of other game. If you wish to produce a pheasant, quail, duck or goose stock, simply substitute the desired bones and trimmings of equal weight. Add Rosemary, Tarragon, and Sage (1/4 Teaspoon of each) to the herb sachet. For rabbit stock, add fennel to the herb sachet. The other ingredients and procedures will stay the same.

Ingredients:
- 10 –12 Pounds of Venison or Elk Bones
- 10 –12 Quarts of Cold Water
- (Items for the Vegetable Mirepoix)
- 1 Pound of Chopped Onion
- 8 Oz of Chopped Carrot
- 8 Oz of Chopped Celery
- 1 Pound of Chopped Tomatoes or Tomato Puree
- (Items for the Sachet or Herb Pouch)

1 Bay Leaf
¼ Teaspoon of Thyme
¼ Teaspoon of Whole Black Peppercorns
8 Parsley Stems
2 Whole Cloves

Special Items or Tools for Cooking: Cheesecloth, string

Preparation: If the venison or elk bones are whole, cut into 3 – 4 inch pieces with a small meat saw. Rinse the bones lightly in cold water. Place the bones into a roasting pan, and place into the oven. Brown at 400 degrees, and brown them well. After the bones have browned, remove from the oven, place them into the stockpot, cover them with cold water, and begin to simmer. Begin to skim, and let the stock continue to simmer. Drain and save the drippings and fats from the roasting pan. Heat the roasting pan on top of the stove, add ½ cup of water to the roasting pan and scrape with a spatula to loosen any fats or juices, and add to the stockpot. Place the vegetable mirepoix, the drippings and fat into the roasting pan, and place into a 400-degree oven to brown, stirring, occasionally. Once the vegetable mirepoix is browned, remove from the oven; add to the stockpot, along with the herb sachet and the tomatoes. Simmer and skim for 6 to 8 hours, adding water to keep the bones covered. Remove the stockpot from heat, and strain through your colander and cheesecloth. Place the stock into a pot and cool in an ice water bath. The stock is now ready to refrigerator or freeze. This recipe will produce about two gallons of brown game stock.

BASIC GAME FISH STOCK

Ingredients: 4 – 6 Pounds of Game Fish Bones (Lean fish and bones are the best)
1 Oz of Butter

8 Oz Dry White Wine
1 Gallon Cold Water
(Items for the Vegetable Mirepoix)
4 Oz Onion (Finely Chopped)
2 Oz Celery (Finely Chopped)
2 Oz Carrot (Finely Chopped)
2 Oz Mushrooms (Chopped)
(Items for the Sachet or Herb Pouch)
½ Bay Leaf
¼ Teaspoon of Black Peppercorns
8 Parsley Stems
1 Whole Clove

Special Items or Tools for cooking: Cheesecloth, string, Bakers Parchment

Preparation: When using fish, ensure that the fish have been scaled and cleaned. You will want to remove the heads and tails before adding the fish to the stockpot. Rinse the fish lightly to remove any excess debris, and pat dry. Place butter into the stockpot, and slowly melt. Next, place the mirepoix into the stockpot, with the bones over the top of the mirepoix. Cover the bones loosely with the bakers' parchment. Cut the paper into a "round" that will fit into the stockpot by tracing the lid of the stockpot and trimming with scissors. Keep the stockpot over low heat for about 5 minutes, or until the bones become opaque in appearance, and begin to "sweat" some of their juices. Remove the parchment, add the wine, and bring to a simmer, then add the water. When the stock begins to simmer, add the herb sachet and begin the skimming process. You will want to simmer this stock for 45 minutes to 1 hour. Do not allow this stock to over cook. Remove the stockpot from the heat, and strain through the colander or china cap lined with cheesecloth. Allow the stock to cool in the ice water bath, and prepare to refrigerate or freeze. This recipe will produce about 1 gallon of fresh game fish stock. If you wish to produce a more concentrated and flavorful fish stock, you may use the method as preparing a white stock, due to sweating the mirepoix and bones in butter and by adding wine.

BASIC AND UNIVERSAL VEGETABLE STOCK

Vegetable stock is the universal and most useable stock to produce for home gourmet cooking, as well as being the simplest to produce. Vegetable stock may be rendered in two hours, and can be used in almost every recipe that you can imagine. During hunting and the holiday season, I always have at least 2 gallons of stock in the freezer or refrigerator at any given time. Vegetable stock is the base for countless soups, stews sauces and gravies. I use it for basting, as a base for rice and vegetable dishes, for enhancing flavors, and as a building block for simple recipes that I wish to take to a higher level of flavor. Weather you are a sportsman, or you purchase your game form a local vendor, vegetable stock is a "must have" in any household that practices the "gourmet arts".

Ingredients:
4 Oz cooking oil
2 Tablespoons Butter
2 Gallons of Water
8 Oz Chopped Onion
8 Oz of Chopped Leeks, (green and white parts)
4 Oz of Chopped Celery
4 Oz of Finely Chopped Cabbage
4 Oz of Chopped Carrots
4 Oz of Chopped Tomatoes, Seeded
1 Large Tablespoon of Chopped Garlic
4 Oz of Finely Chopped Turnip (Optional)
(Ingredients for the Sachet or Herb Pouch)
2 Whole Bay Leaves
½ Teaspoon Thyme
½ Teaspoon Whole Black Peppercorns
12 Parsley Stems (Chopped)

4 Whole Cloves
1 Teaspoon of Fennel Seeds
1 Teaspoon Basil (Optional)

Special Items or Tools for Cooking: Cheesecloth, Colander or China Cap, String
Preparation: Chop all vegetables into medium sized cuts. Add the oil and butter to your stockpot, and heat slowly. Add your vegetables to the stockpot and slowly allow them to "sweat" for five to ten minutes, slowly stirring, so as not to burn or scorch. Add the water and the sachet, or "herb pouch", and simmer for 45 minutes to 1 hour. You do not have to skim this stock, as there is no animal fats or materials produced. Remove the stockpot from the heat, and strain through the colander or china cap, with the layered cheesecloth. Allow stock to cool in an ice water bath. You may now refrigerate or freeze your stock.

BASIC BOUILLON RECIPE, WITH WINE VARIATIONS

Bouillon, is the French word for broth. Bouillon is an ingredient in soups, stews, and is needed in a variety of dishes that call for broth to be used as a base liquid. The recipe for Bouillon included in this chapter, is a Chef's standard recipe. I have also included the white and red wine variations of Bouillon. For the wine variations, do not add vinegar; reduce the amount of water needed by half, adding wine to make up the difference in water. When using wines, use a dry white or dry red wine.

Ingredients: 4 Quarts of Water
1 Cup of White Vinegar
2 Oz of Kosher Salt
12 Oz of Sliced Carrots (Washed and un-peeled)
1 Pound of Onions, Chopped and Peeled

Pinch of Thyme
3 to 4 Whole Bay Leaves
1 Bunch of Parsley Stems (Whole)
½ Oz of Whole Black Peppercorns

Preparation: Add all ingredients in a stockpot, except the peppercorns. Begin to simmer for 1 hour. After 45 minutes, add the peppercorns, and continue to simmer for the remaining 15 minutes. You may need to add additional liquid during the cooking process. If using the vinegar method add an additional quart of water. If using the wine variation, use ½ quart of water. It is important to add all wine at the beginning of the cooking process, allowing time to reduce, and concentrate the flavors. After 1 hour, remove the stockpot from heat, strain through a colander or china cap lined with cheesecloth, and allow Bouillon to cool in an ice water bath. Your Bouillon is now ready to refrigerate or freeze. This recipe will produce about 1 gallon of fresh Bouillon.

Helpful hints from the Chef.

Always attempt to use the freshest ingredients available. Yes, freshness does effect taste! Ensure that your meats, fowl, birds and fish are held at an acceptable, cold temperature. It only takes a few minutes for bacteria to begin to grow.

Inspect all cooking ingredients for freshness or signs of spoilage. Remember that you are going to eat this!

When cutting meat and vegetables on a cutting board or surface, always cut the vegetables first. You must always remember that bacteria from raw meats will make you very sick, or worse! Always clean your cutting boards and knives with a cap full of bleach diluted in a quart of hot water to insure that surfaces are sanitized and free of harmful bacteria!

Always use a "grip", or damp towel under your cutting board to stabilize the cutting surface. A towel will also catch any juices that run off the cutting board. After use, wipe your cutting area with a clean wash rag. Do not use the grip or towel that contains run-off or blood. This will spread bacteria, and contaminate your work area.

Always be sure that the tools you use in any food preparation are sharp, clean and serviceable. A moment of common sense prevention will prevent a trip to the Emergency Room!

SAUCES, GRAVIES, VINAIGRETTES AND TOPPERS

Many components comprise a "complete" meal. When preparing a menu, I have always made it a practice to break the meal down into its many parts. I shape the direction I wish to guide the meal. I plan the flavors that I wish my guests to experience, designing the plate presentation to please both the eye, as well as the pallet. Many times, home gourmets will bury their guests with the latest recipes and taste sensations, that do not blend well, or simple do not go together.

When do we create and use a sauce? Some of the following qualities define the use of sauces when deciding whether to use a sauce or gravy with a dish. Sauces add moisture, flavor, richness and texture; they add to the presentation and appearance of the dish, as well as adding a degree of over all appeal.

It is a learning process to discover what goes with what. If you were serving pizza, would you serve pate as an appetizer? Learning to balance and blend flavors to enhance a dish is an art form that chefs battle with every day. Many times, I have read comments by patrons that would say that the meal was superb, but the sauce was a disaster. It destroyed the flavor of the dish, it was not visually appealing, or it was "dead on arrival".

There are a few simple rules that I have always attempted to apply when creating a dish. Can the main course stand alone, or do I carry it to a higher level by presenting it with a sauce? Will the sauce enhance the flavor, neutralize the flavor, or bury the flavor of the main dish? Will the sauce add to the presentation of the dish, or will it be too much? Will the sauce hold well, or will it look like tar on an Alabama back road in July?!

There is a considerable amount of thought in planning a meal. Not every recipe that I present to you in this book has to soak in sauce or gravy. Most cooking shows tend to present main dishes with an accompanying sauce because they look "pretty". What they neglect to mention is that sauces and gravies can be as delicate as a rosebud, and are very labor intensive. When prepared on television, it appears as simple as tearing open a packet, dump in some wine and water, whisk and serve. There is a degree of chemistry and physics that must be understood and applied to make sauces work. I will not begin to delve into the magic of sauce production at that level! Some things in this world should remain a mystery. Therefore, let us focus the basics. A sauce, by simple definition is a flavored liquid. A sauce is usually, thickened. A sauce is, used to enhance or complement the flavor of foods, vegetables, or desserts.

There are five basic "mother sauces" or base sauces from which all sauces grow. The five mother sauces are White sauce, Brown sauce, or milk sauce, Tomato sauce or Red Sauce, and a Hollandaise or clarified butter sauce. If you have learned how to produce good stocks, as explained in the proceeding chapter, then you shall produce superb sauces.

Three items must exist when producing good sauces. One is stock. I can not emphasize this point too often. If you wish to produce an exceptional sauce, you must have a good stock. Second, you must use fresh ingredients. Ingredients will effect the flavor. There will be times, when substitutions in sauces are necessary. Availability or, lack of ingredients is the usual reason for substitutions. There is not a chef in the world that has not walked to his pantry, reached for an ingredient, and discovered a hole, where their ingredients use to be. That is when a chef creates, or sends his cook to the store! Some of the best sauces that I have ever tasted have been the result of fast thinking and substitutions! The third requirement for a great sauce is patience. This is the most crucial ingredient of all. I was told a long time ago by a chef that to rush a sauce, is to rush nature. Some things must come in there own good time. Never a truer statement was uttered.

In this world of fast food, instant everything, microwaves, and "I want it now" attitudes, cooking and dining have taken the bullet of expediency. People want to eat, not dine. People expect a chef to simply open a can, pour magic onto a plate, and sell it at $6.95!

When you prepare a simple sauce, it may, be prepared quickly. As the sauce becomes more complex so does the production of that sauce. Do not expect perfection in five minutes. It takes time to learn the subtle art of sauces. If you fail, try again! If a chef ever says that he has never ruined or produced a bad sauce, roll up your britches and head for the door!

Gravy is different from a sauce, in that the essential components for gravy are the remaining natural juices from the roasting process, which remain behind in the pan. Less complex then sauces, the results can be as grand in flavor. The juice is removed from the pan, boiled or reduced down to concentrate the flavor, and flour is added along with stock, wine or water, and seasoned. Again, I will attempt to stick to the basic principles in this chapter.

A Demi-glaze is created when you use a rich flavored,well colored brown stock, and combine a dark brown roux, and slowly reduce the liquid, stiring, until it begins to thicken to a desired consistency. Before the demi-glace is fully formed, you then add your herbs, or aromatics, or other ingredients and garnishes.

Vinaigrettes are a blending of vinegars, oils, herbs and spices, that may be served hot or cold. Vinaigrettes are usually considered as a "salad dressing". This is not true. Vinaigrettes may be prepared for a variety of foods. It will add an entirely new dimension to most dishes, and is very healthy to boot!

Toppers, is a general slang term for chutney's, mustards, relishes, salsas and condiments, that accent a dish with a unique and individual flavor. These items, may be served, on the side, or may accompany the main dish, "on top". A good example is freshly prepared horseradish, with prime rib. I have included a few of these recipes in this chapter.

Coulis, are similar to a demi-glace, and are very concentrated in flavor. A coulis is not a difficult sauce to master, but can be very time consuming. A coulis may also be prepared by reducing fruit, and straining it through a sieve, removing all matter, leaving a smooth, refined liquid. These are the types of "desert Coulis" that I have included in this chapter. They are very simple to produce, and are fantastic with desserts!

What are the most common items used to thicken sauces? The most common is cornstarch. Mixed with cool water, it is added to the sauce in small amounts to "tighten" a sauce to its proper thickness. Remember; always add cold to hot to allow the cooking process to bind your sauce together. Always create a smooth mixture when using cornstarch, to prevent lumps.
Flour is the next common thickener. Flour is more difficult to work with as a thickening agent. Flour is sifted into the sauce. The flour is worked into the sauce. Whisk to blend and mix the sauce to produce an even texture.

The next common thickener is the true gourmet's favorite, a Roux. A roux is an equal mixture (by weight) of fat or unsalted butter and flour. A roux is then cooked to produce one of the 3 rouxes. They are a white roux, a blonde roux and a brown roux. Cooking time determines what color or type of roux you produce. A roux is very stable and produced in small amounts to use as desired.

Some regional recipes depend on rouxes more heavily than others. If you have ever read a rue Cajun or Creole cookbook, every other recipe calls for roux. It is a joke in some kitchens that to make cookies in Louisiana, first you get some roux. To make a cake, get some roux. To boil water, first you get some roux! I have included the recipe and technique of how to produce roux in this chapter.

I plan to produce a book entirely devoted to sauces for wild game. It is still in the planning stages, and due to the complexity of developing sauces for game dishes; it will take some time. I have included a number of sauces in this chapter, which will allow you to get a hold of the basics. If it sounds as if I am one of those "snobbish chefs", who does not wish to divulge any trade secrets; please, this is not the case.

There are many aspects of the culinary arts, that require years of study to master. It is a daily chore to gain knowledge. I wish to impart any experience and knowledge I have to all budding gourmets. I wish to teach you the easiest methods possible. I want you to learn and enjoy the art of cooking. I want you to practice, and have the skills to play, and to have fun! If I were to produce a cookbook that read like stereo instructions, then I would have failed at my task.

BASIC ROUX: WHITE, BLONDE & BROWN

To produce a good roux will allow you to produce a good sauce. To make a simple roux requires the following kitchen items. A large saucepan, a wooden spoon, a small scale, graduated measuring cups, flour and unsalted butter.

Ingredients: 6 Oz. Butter, Unsalted
6 Oz. Flour

Preparation: Place the saucepan on the heat source, and slowly melt the butter. If you wish to produce a white or blonde roux, medium heat is required. White roux is "cooked" on medium heat for a few minutes. White roux should only cook long enough to eliminate the "raw flour taste". White Roux should have a chalk like, slightly gritty appearance. White Roux is not pure white in color. When cooked, it has a slight pale yellow color. This color is due to the color of the butter. White roux, is predominantly used, to create Milk Based Sauces, and Béchamel Sauces.

To produce a Blonde Roux, repeat the process for a White Roux, and cook the roux a little longer. A Blonde Roux has the color of ivory, which will produce a sauce of similar color. A technique used to determine that your roux is cooking properly, is the cooking roux will produce a smell resembling a "light, nutty" scent. This roux is used in sauces that are based on white stocks.

To produce a Brown Roux, you must reduce the heat to low. You do not want to scorch the roux. Repeat the above procedures for a white or brown roux. To produce a brown roux requires a little more time. The roux will develop a light brown color, and a "richer, nutty" smell. If you wish to produce a deeper color roux, you may brown the flour in the oven before adding to the butter. Brown roux has less thickening quality then lighter roux's. If necessary, produce a little more brown roux, then a particular recipe calls for, to be safe.

A few suggestions from the Chef for Producing and using Rouxes:

Use a wooded spoon when making a roux.

To develop your skills in blending a roux, use hot water. Chefs use this training technique. This will allow you to practice and hone your skills, without using your stocks, and other ingredients.

Roux is a versatile medium to work with. Liquids may be added to a roux. Roux may be added to liquids.

Liquids may be hot or cool. Do not attempt to blend roux with a cold liquid. It will cause the fats to become solid, producing lumpy sauces.

Roux should be "room temperature" for best results for producing a smooth sauce.

Avoid using aluminum pans and whisks. These tools will actually turn your sauce "gray", due to chemical reaction.

When adding roux to a liquid, the liquid should be simmering, not boiling. Add small amounts of roux to prevent "over thickening", and avoid lumps by "whipping vigorously".

When you add liquids to a roux, re-heat the roux slowly. Use a heavy saucepan to prevent scorching. When the roux is warm, slowly pour the liquid into the pan in small amounts and whip vigorously to prevent lumps.

Please remember to allow the roux/sauce to simmer for a longer amount of time then other sauces. It takes a longer amount of time for a roux thickened sauce to set.

If a sauce requires a longer amount of time to cook or simmer, add less roux. The sauce will naturally thicken as it reduces in volume.

COMPOUND BUTTER FOR ANY OCCASION

Compound Butter is a simple food item to prepare. Compound butter; can be produced to accompany any bread or food. Use unsalted butter. Salted butter may affect the flavor of your compound butter, simply by containing salt. If you are preparing a fish main dish, produce a lemon-herb butter to top your fish. If you bake fresh pesto bread, produce a basil/rosemary butter to accompany the bread. The sky is the limit, bound only by your imagination.

FRESH PESTO BUTTER

When making your compound Butter, use a whip for best results.

Ingredients: ¼ Pound of Unsalted Butter
¼ Teaspoon of Fresh Basil, Finely Minced
¼ Teaspoon of Fresh Rosemary, Finely Minced
¼ Teaspoon of Fresh Thyme, Finely Minced
¼ Teaspoon of Fresh Oregano, Finely Minced
¼ Teaspoon of Fresh Tarragon, Finely Minced
¼ Teaspoon of Fresh Parsley, Finely Minced
¼ Teaspoon of Garlic Powder
¼ Teaspoon of Freshly Cracked Black Pepper

Preparation: Place butter into a mixing bowl and allow to soften. When butter is workable and soft, break butter apart with a rubber spatula, add all ingredients, and whip vigorously with a wire whip, whisk, or mixer. Blend all ingredients thoroughly and evenly. When all components are blended, use a rubber scrapper to remove butter from bowl, and place on a 12-inch long sheet of wax paper, or plastic wrap. Form butter into the shape of a log, allowing room on the ends to twist and compress the butter. Slowly begin to role and form the butter into a dense, firm log. When rolling is complete, twist the ends tightly, adding pressure to compress the butter. Using a small piece of tape, secure the middle, and ends to prevent opening. Place compound butter into the refrigerator or freezer to firm.

When needed, remove the butter, and slice into ¼ inch thick medallions and serve on the side, directly on the dish, or on top of a vegetable dish. Compound butter may be placed on the top of soups, to accent and richen their flavor.

TRADITONAL ALMOND BUTTER

This compound butter is superb with fish or vegetable dishes.

Ingredients: ½ Cup of Almonds, Peeled and Toasted
½ Pound of Unsalted Butter
1 Tablespoon of Almond Oil or Extract

Preparation: Placed almonds on a cutting board and chop into small pieces. Place chopped almonds on a small pan, and place into the oven to toast (325 degrees for 5 to 10 minutes). When almonds are toasted, remove and place into a food processor or blender, add almond oil or extract and puree. You will create a smooth concentrated almond paste. Remove paste, and add to soft butter. Mix evenly and thoroughly. If you wish to intensify the taste, add additional almond paste or oil in small amounts. Remove butter, form, roll chill and serve.

TRADITIONAL GARLIC & CHIVE BUTTER

This recipe is excellent for soups, fish, game, fowl or vegetables. Know to some as "snail butter", this recipe is universal in its name, and uses. This is also a great butter to use for garlic bread.

Ingredients: ¼ Pound of Unsalted butter
1 Tablespoon of Unsalted Butter
2 Tablespoons of Fresh Minced Garlic
2 Tablespoons of Finely Minced, Fresh Chives

Preparation: Slowly melt butter in a small skillet, add the minced garlic and sauté for 5 minutes. When the garlic is soft and sweet, remove from heat, stir in the fresh chives, and allow to cool. Place butter into a bowl to soften. Using a rubber spatula, break apart the butter. Add the cool garlic and chives, and whip vigorously to blend. When evenly blended, remove from bowl, form, roll chill and serve.

STEAK BUTTER OR "MAITRE d' BUTTER"

A traditional compound butter recipe that is an excellent choice for large game dishes and steaks. This is a "must" for any household that is considered a "steak and potatoes home".

Ingredients:
- ½ Pound of Unsalted Butter
- 4 Tablespoons of Fresh, Finely Chopped Parsley
- 2 Tablespoons of Fresh Lemon Juice
- ¼ Teaspoon of Kosher Salt
- 2 Teaspoons Fresh Cracked Black Pepper
- 1 Teaspoon of Spicy Mustard

Preparation: Allow Butter to soften in a mixing bowl. Use a rubber spatula to break the butter into smaller pieces. Combine all ingredients and whip vigorously to blend evenly. Remove butter from bowl with a rubber scraper, shape form, roll chill, slice and serve.

SPICY CREOLE MUSTARD BUTTER

This butter is wonderful for grilled meats and vegetables. When you want to add a hot and wild flavor to a grilled dish, this is the compound butter to use!

Ingredients: ½ Pound of Unsalted Butter
3 Tablespoons Dijon-style Mustard
½ Tablespoon of Fresh Cracked Black Pepper
½ Teaspoon of Cayenne Pepper
½ Teaspoon of Garlic Powder
½ Teaspoon of Onion Powder
½ Teaspoon Chili Powder
½ Teaspoon of Hot Sauce

Preparation: Place butter into a mixing bowl and allow to soften. When butter is soft, use a rubber spatula to break butter into small pieces. Add all ingredients, and whip vigorously, blending all ingredients. Remove butter from bowl with a rubber scraper, shape, form, roll, chill, slice and serve.

VINAIGRETTES SAUCES, GRAVIES, VINAIGRETTES AND TOPPERS

Vinaigrette, is one of the truly simplistic gourmet items that you can produce at home. Some of the commonly asked questions about vinaigrettes, "Are there basic formulas for vinaigrettes?" The answer is yes! There is a basic vinaigrette recipe. "What can you do with a vinaigrette?" Most vinaigrette is served with salads and chilled vegetable dishes. I have heated vinaigrettes, served them with pasta, vegetables, wilted salads and used vinaigrettes for marinades. I will suggest to you, the home gourmet to decide what you like, and expand on those recipes. "How many vinaigrette recipes or variations are there?" The only answer is countless variations! As I have stated before, "Food and cooking is only confined by the imagination of the person preparing the dish." By substituting different oils, different seasonings and spices, you will create hundreds of variations and recipes. When you know the basics of cooking, you can learn to create the food of the gods! I present to you five of my favorite recipes.

ANY CHEF'S BASIC VINAIGRETTE

Ingredients:
1-Cup Olive Oil (any type of basic olive is fine)
1/3 Cup of White or Red Wine Vinegar
¼ Teaspoon of White Pepper
1/8 Teaspoon of Fine Kosher Salt

Preparation: Combine all ingredients in a mixing bowl, and vigorously whip until blended. Place into a small decanter and chill for 1 hour. Shake well before serving.

CILANTRO & LIME VINIAGRETTE

Ingredients:
1-Cup Olive Oil (any olive oil is fine)
¼ Cup of "Sparkling or Champagne" Vinegar
1/3 Cup Fresh Lime Juice
1 Small Jalapeno Pepper
1 Small Serrano Pepper
½ Cup Fresh Cilantro, (leaves only)
½ Teaspoon Garlic Powder
½ Teaspoon Fresh Cracked Black Pepper
½ Teaspoon Kosher Salt
1 Tablespoon Black Olives (drained & chopped)

Preparation: Clean and de-seed the Serrano and Jalapeno peppers, chopping them into small pieces. Pluck and de-stem the fresh Cilantro leaves, rinse and pat dry. Place all the ingredients into a blender and blend on the puree setting. Place into a container and allow to "sweat" for at least 1 hour. Shake well and serve.

VINAIGRETTE WITH SUN-DRIED TOMATOES

This is another of my household favorites. I have always enjoyed the "bite" of sun-dried tomatoes, and usually have a five-pound bag in my pantry at any time!

Ingredients:
½ Cup Sun-dried Tomatoes
2 Cups of Olive Oil
2/3 Cups Red Wine Vinegar
4 Tablespoons of Cool Water
2 Small Green Onions, (tops and bottoms, Chopped)
1 Tablespoon Fresh Parsley (tops only, Chopped)
1 Tablespoon Fresh Basil, Chopped
¼ Teaspoon of Kosher Salt
¼ Teaspoon of Fresh Cracked Black Pepper

Preparation: Place sun-dried tomatoes and olive oil in a small glass bowl and allow tomatoes to soak for 3 hours. Remove the sun-dried tomatoes, drain the olive into the bowl, and finely mince the sun-dried tomatoes on a small cutting board. Place all ingredients (including olive oil) into a blender or food processor and puree. Add the sun-dried tomatoes to the finished mixture, place into a container, and let stand for 1 hour. Shake well and serve.

FAR-EAST ORIENTAL VINAIGRETTE

When you want a taste of the orient, use this vinaigrette. A chef that I worked with taught me this recipe. It has been a favorite ever since.

Ingredients: 2 Cups of Peanut Oil
4 Tablespoons of Soy Sauce
2 Tablespoons of Sesame Oil
½ Cup of Rice Wine Vinegar
1 & ½ Tablespoons of Garlic, Finely Minced
1 Level Tablespoon of Ginger Powder, (or two Tablespoons of fresh, grated Ginger Root)
2 Tablespoons of Green Onion Tops, Finely Chopped)
1 Teaspoon of Lime Juice

Preparation: Place 1 tablespoon of peanut oil into a small skillet, and heat slowly. Add the minced garlic, and slowly sauté until the garlic is soft and tender. Place all other ingredients into a blender or food processor and puree for 30 seconds. Add the sautéed garlic, and puree for another 30 seconds, until the contents are well blended. Remove, place into a small container, and allow to "rest" for 1 hour. Shake well and serve.

I have used this vinaigrette as a marinade for fish and game birds by adding 1 large tablespoon of orange juice concentrate, and 2 tablespoons of Teriyaki Sauce. Allow meat to soak for 3 hours, and fish to soak for one to two hours, then grill!

BASIC RED WINE VINAIGRETTE WITH GARLIC & ONION

A simple recipe that goes well with a large summer mixed field-greens salad, freshly toasted baguette bread with olive oil and red pepper!

Ingredients: 2 Cups Olive Oil

½ Cup of Red Wine Vinegar
½ Cup of any Dry Red Wine
1 Tablespoon of Fresh Garlic, Finely Chopped
1 Large Green Onion, Tops & Bottoms, Chopped
¼ Teaspoon of Kosher Salt
½ Teaspoon of Fresh Cracked Black Pepper
1 Tablespoon of Fresh Chopped Parsley

Preparation: Place 1 tablespoon of olive oil and garlic into a small skillet and slowly sauté for 5 minutes. Place all other ingredients into a blender or food processor. Add garlic and puree for one to two minutes, blending contents. Place contents into a container, and refrigerate for one hour. Shake well and serve!

MANGO CHUTNEY FOR GRILLED FISH

A sauté chef that worked for me a while ago was crazy for chutneys! She created this recipe, and it was great with seared tuna, and large fillets of game fish. This chutney has a flavorful blend of sweet and spicy, that create a hot and wild flavor all its own!

Ingredients: 4 Cups Fresh Peeled and Large Diced Mango
½ Cup Sugar
½ Cup Water
¼ Cup White Wine Vinegar
¼ Cup Pecans, Finely Chopped
1 Tbsp. Fresh Mint, Finely Chopped
1 Tsp. Lime Juice
1 Tsp. Fresh Cracked Black Pepper

Preparation; Add water, sugar, vinegar to a covered sauce pan and bring to simmer. Add the mango and simmer for 30 minutes. Add the remaining ingredients and allow to simmer for an additional 10 minutes. Chill or serve warm.

AVOCADO RELISH

Ingredients:
4 Ripe Avocados, Peeled, Seeded, Chopped
3 Serrano Peppers, Seeded, Finely Chopped
4 Tbsp. Fresh Cilantro, Finely Chopped
1 Small Onion, Finely Chopped
3 Roma Tomatoes, Finely Chopped
2 Tbsp. Lime Juice
1 Tbsp. Lemon Juice
1 Tbsp. Tequila
1 Tsp. Garlic Salt
1 Tbsp. Black Pepper
1 Tsp. Olive Oil

Preparation: Mix in a glass or plastic bowl. Mix slowly and gently. Refrigerate for at least 45 minutes. Serve chilled.

SOUTHWESTERN PICO De GALLO

A traditional Southwestern favorites that is used on every thing form eggs to Fajitas! I would consider this as a universal topper for any wild game or domestic meat, fish or fowl. I keep a fresh batch of Pico in my refrigerator at all times!

Ingredients:
2 Cups Roma Tomatoes, Chopped
2 Cups Onion, Diced
4 Serrano Peppers, Remove seeds, Minced
1 Tsp. Lemon Juice

1 Tsp. Lime Juice
1 Tsp. Cracked Black Pepper
½ Bunch Cilantro, Chopped

Preparation: Place all ingredients into a plastic container with lid. Refrigerate and shake occasionally to evenly mix. Chill for at least 45 minutes. Serve chilled.

CRACKED BLACK PEPPER SAUCE

This sauce is designed for use with most game dishes. Prepare this sauce and use on desired cuts of game

Ingredients:
1 Tbsp. Vegetable Oil
2 Tbsp. Bacon, finely diced
1 Small Carrot, peeled and grated
1 Small White Onion, Finely chopped
1 Tbsp. Garlic, Minced
1 Tbsp. Fresh Parsley, Chopped
1 Tbsp. Fresh Thyme, Chopped
1 Bay Leaf, Ground
¼ Cup White Wine Vinegar
½ Cup Dry White Wine
1 Tbsp. Cracked Black Pepper
1 ½ Cup Game Stock
2 Tbsp. Brown Roux

Preparation: In a large sauté pan, add bacon and cook until light and tender. Add carrot, onion, and oil stirring until vegetable are soft. Add garlic and herbs and spices and continue to sauté for 10 minutes. Add vinegar ad wine and reduce by 2/3. Add black pepper and thickened game stock with roux and continue to simmer until desired thickness is achieved. Add 2 tablespoons butter and mix together. Strain sauce through fine sieve and serve.

GINGER AND LIME SAUCE

This sauce is another multi-purpose sauce that may be applied to many different game dishes.

Ingredients:
4 Tbsp. Fresh Grated Ginger
2 Small Green Onions, Minced
1 Tbsp. Parsley, Chopped
1 Cup White Wine
¼ Cup Fresh Lime Juice
2 Tbsp. Fresh Lime Zest
1 Tsp. Kosher Salt
1 Tsp. White Pepper
½ Lb. Unsalted Butter, cut into small cubes

Preparation: In a small sauce pan, blanch lime zest in lightly salted for 3-5 minutes then strain. In another sauce pan, simmer ginger, onion, parsley and wine until reduced by 2/3. Add lime juice and simmer for 5-10 additional minutes. Strain through a fine sieve. Return to pan and begin to simmer add lime zest and stir in small amounts of butter until thickened and serve.

HONEY BAR-B-QUE SAUCE

A traditional Bar-B-Que sauce with a slight twist. This sauce will not only hang on to any game meat, but will also hang on to your fingers!

Ingredients:
¼ Cup Game Stock
¼ Cup Unsalted Butter
1 Bunch Green Onions, Minced without tops
2 Tbsp. Garlic, Minced

2 Cups Sweet Catsup
¼ Cup Worchester Sauce
¼ Cup Apple Cider Vinegar
½ Cup Beer
2 Tbsp. Spicy Brown Mustard
4 Tbsp. Brown Sugar
2 Tbsp. Chili Powder
1 Tsp. Cumin
½ Honey

Preparation: In a large sauce pan add game stock, butter, onion, pepper and garlic and slowly simmer for 30 minutes. Remove contents and place in large mixing bowl. Add all remaining ingredients and whisk thoroughly. Cover and refrigerate for 24 hour. Slowly reheat when ready to serve.

ROSEMARY HERB SAUCE

This sauce is another broad usage sauce that may be prepared and served with a variety of wild game dishes.

Ingredients: 4 Tbsp. Unsalted Butter
3 Green Onions, Finely Minced
1 Cup Red Wine
2 Tbsp. Rosemary, Chopped
2 Tbsp. Thyme, Chopped
2 Tbsp. Basil, Chopped
1 Tbsp. Marjoram, Chopped
1 Bay Leaf, Ground
2 Pints Heavy Cream
2 Tbsp. Coarse Ground Mustard
1 Tsp. Kosher Salt
1 Tbsp. Cracked Black Pepper

Preparation: In a sauté pan add butter and slowly sauté onion for 5 minutes. Add Red wine and herbs, and reduce by 2/3. Add heavy cream and continue to simmer until reduced by ½. Stir in mustard, salt and pepper. Add strain through a fine sieve. Place aside and keep warm until ready to serve.

CHILLED HORSERADISH CHUTNEY

This chutney sauce s great with large game. It is a perfect combination of sweet and hot. It has a touch of a tangy under flavor as an added bonus!

Ingredients: 1 Cup Fresh Mango Chutney
1 Cup Horseradish
1 Cup Fresh Pineapple
1 Tsp. Orange Zest

Preparation: Take the horseradish, and place onto a clean, finely woven cotton towel. Twist the towel until all the liquid is pressed from the horseradish. Place horseradish, chutney, pineapple, and orange zest in to food processor and puree until evenly blended and reduced to an even consistency. Place into a covered bowl and serve.

WILD MUSTANG GRAPE AND PECAN CHUTNEY

This is a recipe that a chef in Texas gave to me. He picks the Mustang grapes, and prepares this chutney for his local game dishes I hope you enjoy the topper!

Ingredients: ½ Cup Raisins
2 Oz Brandy

1 Tbsp. Minced Garlic
¼ Tsp. Kosher Salt
¼ Cup Kane Brown Sugar
3 Tbsp. Fresh Lemon Juice
½ Tsp. Dry Mustard
1 Tbsp. Horseradish, Press out the Liquid
1 Tbsp. Fresh Grated Gingerroot
½ Cup Cider Vinegar
3 Cups Fresh Mustang Grapes
2 Cups Fresh Diced Apple
½ Cup Diced Fresh Peach

Preparation: Add the brandy to the raisins, and allow to soak for several hours. Then strain raisins and discard remaining brandy. Combine all ingredients into a saucepan, except the fruit, and bring to a rapid boil, then reduce to a simmer allowing the sugars to dissolve. Add the remaining ingredients, and simmer for an addition 30 to 45 minutes. Remove, place into a bowl, cover, chill and serve.

SIMPLE POLYNESIAN SAUCE

This sauce is as simple and quick as it gets. I was taught how to prepare this sauce by a lady from Hawaii, who had learned it from her mother. It is good!

Ingredients: 1 Quart Fresh Pineapple Juice
2 Cups Fresh Bird or Venison Game Stock
2 Cups Chopped Pineapple
1 Cup Mango
1 Cup Sweet Catsup
1 Tbsp. Garlic Powder
1 Tbsp. Onion Powder

Corn Starch to thicken

Preparation: Add all ingredients (except catsup) into a saucepan and reduce by 1/3 at a boil. When reduced, add the catsup, whisk, and reduce to a simmer for 10 minutes. Thicken with cornstarch, and serve hot.

FRUIT COULIS FOR DESSERTS

Fruit Coulis are simple to produce. I have given you two basic methods to prepare these coulis, and with the exception of your choice of Liquors, their preparation is almost the same.

The key to dessert coulis is to simmer and reduce them slowly. This is a procedure that is best unhurried. Always add the liquor during the last 15 to 30 minutes of reduction, to allow the alcohol time to evaporate. You want to push the reduced mixture thru a fine sieve to remove all left over fruit and residue. The final sauce should be a thick, rich reduction that may be served chilled or warm. I make fruit-liquor coulis in large amounts around the holidays for those quick desert solutions when those unexpected guests drop by.

BLUEBERRY AND GRAND MARNIER COULIS

This coulis is devastating over cheesecake. Ask my wife!

Ingredients: 1 Pint Fresh Blueberries
2 Tbsp. Water
¼ Cup Sugar
1 Tbsp. Fresh Lemon Juice
¼ Tsp. Nutmeg

2 Tbsp. Cornstarch dissolved
3 Oz. Grand Marnier

Preparation: In a saucepan add blueberries, water, sugar, lemon juice and bring to a rapid boil. Reduce heat and simmer for 10- 20 minutes. Add Grand Mariner and simmer for an additional 15 minutes while stirring. Add small amount of water to cornstarch in a small cup. Slow whisk cornstarch into sauce to thicken. Press mixture through a sieve and set aside to cool.

ORANGE BOURBON WHISKEY SAUCE

If you wish to add a bite to your desert, then this is the sauce to prepare. This recipe is a favorite of mine, that goes well over a dish of fresh vanilla ice cream, and has been used with certain fresh chilled fruits. This is a desert sauce to die for!

Ingredients: 2 Cups Brown Sugar
4 Tbsp. Unsalted Butter
1 Cup Fresh squeezed Orange juice, strained
Zest from one large Orange
Zest from ½ Fresh Lemon
½ Cup Bourbon Whiskey

Preparation: In a saucepan, slowly heat butter adding brown sugar and stir until dissolved. Add orange juice and fruit zests blending thoroughly. Add bourbon whiskey blend and bring to a simmer for 10 minutes. Sauce should be smooth in texture. Remove form heat and serve warm.

SMALL GAME, CRITTERS AND VARMINTS!

Small game is a delicacy waiting to happen. Most hunters and sportsmen consider small game as a second string, or less then quality type of game meat. Most small game is considered, as backwoods food. It is lumped into an unflattering grouping of "Critters and Varmints". I can not disagree, more. Granted, small game does not look as impressive mounted on your trophy room wall. When viewed in a sauté pan, or baking in a slow oven, those under represented game animals make up in taste and flavor, for what they lack in size and stature!

Many people view small game with a very narrow scope. Most individuals, if asked to prepare small game could name rabbit and squirrel, and then draw a blank. If you suggested any number of other small game animals (woodchuck, beaver, raccoon, opossum, armadillo) you would hear the usual answer of "I could not possibly eat that!" How little the public truly understands about small game and what preconceived notions individuals have about wild game, or food in general.

I have resorted to slight of hand on a several occasions. I would invite a few friends over to dinner. I would not disclose what the main course was going to be. I would engage them in some discussion about "gourmet dishes" and then surprise them with a sumptuous main course. After dinner, I would slowly clue them in on what the meat was, how it was prepared and sauced. The usual reaction was "I would have never guessed that was raccoon. I thought raccoons were big rodents, and carried diseases!" A small amount of misinformation is deadly.

Small game will provide the at home wild game gourmet with a vast number of culinary opportunities, if the game meat is handled, prepared and cooked correctly. When small game is cleaned, marinated seasoned and cooked with loving care, you shall discover what many chefs and game cooks have realized for years. Small game can produce some of the biggest of flavors!

These few tips and recommendations for preparing and cooking small game should help you get started if you are a novice in this area of game cooking. When selecting, or hunting small game, you should apply the same standards to them as you would other game animals. Young small game, in good condition will provide the choicest meats, and the best of flavors. As small game ages, so does the flavor, and texture of the meat. Normally rabbit and squirrel have the best of flavor and texture. These small game animals have the subtlest of wild game flavors, and are by far the most versatile when it is time to prepare and cook them. When I was in Europe, rabbit was a true gourmet dish, and was preferred in many cases to beef!

If you do bag an older, tougher small game animal, there are several ways to soften their meat, and remove a large amount of their "gamy" flavor. The first method is lightly parboiling your game meat. This will tenderize them and if you add a small amount of wine or vinegar to the parboiling process, you will eliminate a lot of the "gamy flavor" from the meat. The preferred method is to perform a "long marinade" and include in the marinade some pineapple, papaya or mango juice. These juices will quickly break down the tissue and muscle fiber. These juices will actually dissolve meat and tissue. Please monitor the marinating process, and do not let your small game soak for more then 12 to 24 hours.

When cooking small game, several cooking methods can be applied, depending on the age and toughness or condition of the animal, and what the recipe advises. When preparing young, tender small game animals, slow dry heat, or a slow oven is preferred. Slow sautéing, lightly searing, and covered baking and broiling are also favored. Be advised that small game also require a small amount of fat or "larding" to prevent the game meat from becoming too dry during the cooking process.

If the game is less tender, and the small game is older, then you might consider preparing your dish by stewing, slow simmering, or a slow braising method. The moister the heat, the better for older, less tender game animals. I would also adjust your cooking time for small game if the meat were less tender. You always want to monitor your cooking time as not to over cook, or dry the meat out. Baste or re-wet as often as necessary, using the juices and fats in the pan, of by preparing a basting marinade with additional fats or butter.

When seasoning your small game, use the less is principal. When seasoning small game in a stew or other wet cooking method, season lightly, and taste often. You always wish to combine the natural game flavors and seasonings to produce a taste that is not over powering or to strong. Season with reason, when working with small game.

HONEY GLAZED SQUIRREL WITH GINGER

This is a slight variation of Far East flavors. Since rabbit and squirrel are the most adaptable of game meats, then most conventional recipes may be applied. I recommend serving this dish with the wild game stock, rice pilaf recipe included in Chapter Side Dishes.

Ingredients: 3 Large, young squirrel, Cleaned and cut into serving sizes.

2 Tbsp. of Unsalted Butter
½ Cup Honey
¼ Cup of Chopped Green Onion
¼ Cup Fresh Vegetable Stock
1 Tsp. Zested Fresh Orange Peel
1 Tsp. Kosher Salt
1 Tbsp. Fresh Ginger
1 Tsp. Of Minced Garlic
1 Tsp. Fresh Cracked Black Pepper

Marinade Ingredients
2 Cups Water
¼ Cup Teriyaki Sauce
1 Tbsp. Soy Sauce
1 Tbsp. Ginger Powder
¼ Cup Fresh Orange Juice
1 Tbsp. Fresh Lemon Juice

Preparation: Place cleaned, rinsed and cut squirrel into a large glass bowl. In a separate bowl, blend the marinade, and pour over the squirrel. Turn the meat to ensure an even coating of marinade, cover, and place into the refrigerator for 3 hours. In a small saucepan, slowly melt the butter, then add the fresh vegetable stock, and heat on medium for 5 minutes. Add the remaining ingredients to the saucepan and heat, until evenly blended, and sauce begins to thicken. Remove the squirrel from the refrigerator, remove from the marinade, and shake off the excess marinade. Place the squirrel into a large baking dish, and pour the sauce over the squirrel. Place the squirrel into a 350-degree, oven and bake for 30 minutes, before turning the meat and baking for an additional 30 minutes. Meat should have an internal temperature of 145 degrees or higher, and be tender and moist. Remove squirrel and serve with sauce from baking pan. Garnish with additional orange and lemon zest.

BURGANDY PAN SAUTED SQUIRREL WITH MUSHROOMS

Squirrel is one of the most versatile, and easily adaptable of small game. Its mild game flavor and ability to absorb the seasonings and flavors that are prepared with it, allow squirrel to travel in any direction that your taste buds desire. This is a very simple recipe that is favorable, by its simplicity. When cleaning your squirrel, remember to remove the scent glands for the fore legs.

Ingredients:
- 3 Large young squirrels, cut into serving pieces
- 1 Tsp. Kosher Salt
- 1 Tsp. Fresh Cracked Black Pepper
- 1 Tbsp. Fresh Minced Garlic
- 2 Cups Flour
- 12 Bacon Slices, Diced
- ½ Cup Purple Onion, Diced
- 2 Cups Mushrooms, Sliced
- 1 ½ Cups Burgundy or red wine

Preparation: Clean and rinse squirrel, allowing meat to remain wet. In a bowl, blend flour, salt, and pepper. Dredge squirrel in seasoned flour mixture, insuring to coat evenly and fully. In a large cast iron skillet add bacon and garlic and sauté over low heat until bacon crisp and garlic is tender. Add squirrel and pan sauté with bacon and garlic for 15-20 minutes or until evenly and nicely browned. Add diced onions, sliced mushrooms and wine to skillet. Reduce heat to low and simmer for 1 ½ to 2 hours or until game meat is tender and done. Remove, garnish and sere as desired.

SOUTHERN SMOKED SQUIRREL WITH PECANS

Squirrel was the first game that I ever had the opportunity to hunt, as a small boy. I did not think about cooking them. I was the next Daniel Boone in training, and would set out after school with my single shoot .22 rifle and stalk the woods in search of the vicious wild squirrel. Mom was the chief cook in those days!

3 Whole Squirrel, Cleaned
4 Cups White Wine
1 Cup Soy Sauce
2 Cup Peanut Oil
3 Cup Flour
1-2 Tbsp. Garlic Salt
1 Tbsp. Onion Powder
1 Tbsp. Kosher Salt
1 Tbsp. Cayenne Pepper
1 Tbsp. Fresh Cracked Black Pepper
1 Cup of Very Finely Chopped Pecans
2 Cups Vegetable Oil

In a mixing bowl, combine wine, soy sauce and peanut oil and blend, together. Clean and rinse your squirrel, place into a large, airtight, plastic bag or container, add the marinade. Place into the refrigerator and allow game to marinade 2-3 days. Turn bag occasionally to disperse marinade. Remove squirrel and discard marinade. In a shallow pan, evenly blend the flour, pecans and seasonings. Dredge the squirrel in the seasoned flour, ensuring a full and even coating. Deep-fry the squirrel in oil for 3-5 minutes, to make coating crisp. Place squirrel on a smoker rack and slow smoke for 2 hours. Turn squirrel occasionally, to allow the smoky flavor into impress the meat.

RABBIT VIN BLANC

This is a classic French recipe that is enjoyed by the civilized dining world. I had this dish in Paris a number of years ago, and it was fantastic! I knew a chef who referred to this dish as "drunken bunny on a board". You may now understand why French Chefs do not think highly of American cuisine!

1 Large Rabbit Cut into serving pieces
1 Large White Onion, Thinly Sliced
2 Cups Dry White Wine
1 Cup Flour
1 Cup Vegetable Oil
2 Tbsp. Coarse Ground Black Pepper
1 Tbsp. Kosher Salt
4 Tbsp. Finely Minced Garlic
2 Bay Leaf
3 Tbsp. Olive Oil
1 Cup Sour Cream
2 Cups White Wine Vinegar
2 Cups Water

Place cleaned and cut rabbit in a large glass dish. Combine 1 cup wine, and spices, ½ cup onion, water, and vinegar in equal parts to cover rabbit. Marinate for 2 days, covered in the refrigerator. Remove and pat the rabbit dry. Sprinkle with salt and pepper and then roll in flour. Brown in oil, in a large Dutch oven on medium high heat. In a small saucepan combine 1 cup white wine, garlic and remaining spices with ½ cup onion. Heat on medium high heat for 10 minutes. Add wine sauce to rabbit, reduce heat, and simmer for 20 minutes. Remove rabbit and thicken drippings, slowly adding flour. Add sour cream to Dutch oven and blend evenly just before finishing. Plate rabbit; and pour sour cream and wine sauce over rabbit, garnish and serve.

HASENPFEFFER

I was requested, to include this traditional rabbit recipe in this cookbook. I have always enjoyed this recipe, and am reminded of the first time that I was shown how to prepare this dish. I hope that you enjoy this recipe.

1 Large Rabbit, Cut into 8ths
1 ¼ Cup Flour
½ Tsp. Garlic Powder
1 Tsp. Kosher Salt
1 ½ Tsp. Fresh Cracked Black Pepper
3 Tbsp. Butter
¼ Cup Dry Cooking Sherry
¾ Cup Sour Cream
¾ Cup Red Wine Vinegar
1 ½ Cup Red Wine
1 ¾ Cup Fresh Vegetable Stock
1 Onion, Chopped
½ Cup Celery, Chopped
1 Bay Leaf
¼ Cup Gin

Combine red wine vinegar, ½ cup red wine, ¾ cup stock, onion, celery, bay leaf, gin, ½ teaspoon salt, 1 teaspoon pepper in a large glass dish, and mix thoroughly. Clean, cut and rinse rabbit, place into the marinade and leave covered in the refrigerator for 24 hours. Remove rabbit and pat dry. Mix flour, salt and pepper in a shallow pan. Place rabbit pieces into the flour mixture, coating thoroughly. Melt butter in sauté pan and slowly add rabbit. Add 1 cup red wine and 1 cup stock. Simmer over medium heat for 1 hour. Remove rabbit pieces and place on serving platter and hold warm. Pour pan drippings through a fine sieve to remove solids. Discard solids and reheat pan liquids; reducing over high heat for 10 minutes. Add Sherry and reduce heat to low, and continue to simmer for 4 minutes. Remove from heat and stir in sour cream, blending evenly and smoothly. Pour sauce over rabbit, garnish and serve.

LOUISIANNA CREOLE RABBIT WITH SPICY CREOLE SAUCE

This is a great Louisiana recipe. "It smacks of nuttin but good eatin, ya'll". I was given this recipe several years ago, and it is a great dish to serve on a cold day, near a warm fire. My original recipe notes were titled "Bayou Bunny", and suggests that this game dish be served with "a mess of dirty rice and corn bread". Try this dish with the dirty rice and corn bread recipes included in this book.

Ingredients:
- 3 to 4 Pounds of Fresh cleaned Rabbit
- 1 Cup Milk
- 1 Cup Flour
- 1 Tsp. Kosher Salt
- 1 Tbsp. of Fresh Cracked Black Pepper
- 1 Tsp. Garlic Powder
- 1 Tsp. Onion Powder
- 1 Tsp. Cayenne Pepper
- ¼ Cup of Bacon, Chopped

3 Tbsp. of Peanut Oil

Ingredients for the Creole Sauce

2 Medium Onions, Sliced
½ Cup Green Bell Pepper, Finely Chopped
½ Cup Red Bell Pepper, Finely Chopped
2 Tbsp. Garlic, Finely Minced
1 Tbsp. Fresh Parsley, Chopped
3 Tbsp. Butter
6 oz of Tomato Paste
3 Cups of Tomato Stock, or Juice
¼ Tbsp. Worcestershire Sauce
½ Tsp. Kosher Salt
1 Tbsp. Black Pepper
1 Tbsp. Cayenne Pepper
2 Tbsp. Hot Sauce or Tabasco Sauce
1 Tbsp. Lemon Juice
1 Cup of White Wine

Preparation: Prepare the sauce first. In a large saucepan, add the butter, and slowly heat. Add the garlic, Bell Peppers, Parsley and onions, and sauté until soft and golden brown in color. Add all other ingredients and simmer slowly for 30 minutes, stirring occasionally. Place the rabbit into a bowl and cover with the milk, and refrigerate for one hour. Slowly sauté the bacon in Peanut oil, a large cast iron or oven safe skillet. When bacon is cooked, remove and add to Creole Sauce, reserving the bacon fat and oil. Add spices to the flour and blend, together in a shallow pan. Remove the rabbit from the milk, and dredge in the seasoned flour. Slowly brown the rabbit until golden brown, and pour the Creole Sauce over the rabbit and place into a 325 degree oven for 1 & ½ hours, or until meat is done. Internal temperature should be above 145 degrees. Serve over dirty rice with corn bread.

BAKED RACCOON

When I first prepared this dish my daughter protested not about the meal, but about the fact that raccoons were "cute". I then reminded her as to where coon skin hats come from, and she quickly ceased with her protests!

Ingredients:
- 1 Young, Raccoon, Cleaned and dressed
- 1 Tsp. Red Pepper
- 1 Tsp. Fresh Cracked Black Pepper
- 4 Tbsp. Kosher Salt
- 2 Tbsp. Fresh Minced Garlic
- 1 Cup Red Onion, Sliced
- 2 Cups Fresh Carrots Quartered
- 6 Fresh Medium Potatoes, Quartered
- 1 Cup of Red Wine
- 3 Quarts Water

Preparation: Add 2 tablespoons of salt and red wine to water. Bring to a rapid boil. Add raccoon and continue to slow boil for 30 minutes. Remove raccoon from water and place in shallow baking dish. Blend spices and garlic together, and rub liberally on raccoon. Surround with onions. Cover and bake at 300° for 45 minutes. Place carrots and potatoes in juice and continue to bake until vegetables are tender, about 15-20 additional minutes.

LONE STAR DEEP FRIED RATTLESNAKE with AVOCADO RELISH

I highly recommend that you try this dish. If you wish to present the ultimate of Texas treats, then deep fried rattlesnake is the dish to present. Rattlesnake is served in the finest gourmet restaurants in the Lone Star State, and is considered by many as a Texas signature dish, along with Bar-B-Que. If you ever get to Texas in the spring, go by the Annual Taylor Rattlesnake Round-Up, in Taylor Texas. This is a dish that will not bite back!

Ingedients: 1 Large Dressed Rattlesnake
Marinade:
½ Cup Water
½ Cup Soy Sauce
2 Tbsp. Fresh Lemon Juice
2 Tbsp. Fresh Lime Juice
2 0z. Tequila
2 Tbsp. Garlic
1. Tsp. Black Pepper
1 Tsp. Kosher Salt
Batter:
2 Eggs, Beaten
2/3 Cup Milk
2/3 Cup Flour
1 Tbsp. Hot Sauce
1 Tbsp. Cayenne
1 tsp. Garlic Powder
1 Tsp. Paprika
1 Tsp. Onion Powder
1 Tsp. Black Pepper
3 Cups Peanut Oil

Preparation: Rinse and clean rattlesnake meat and cut into 3-inch pieces. Combine ingredients of marinade in large bowl; blend for 1 minute with whisk. Add rattlesnake and allow to soak for 24 hour, covered in refrigerator. Remove meat from marinade and pat dry. Make batter by combining eggs, milk, flour, hot sauce, cayenne, garlic and onion powder, and black pepper; combine in bowl stir to even batter. In a large Dutch oven add peanut oil; heating on medium high, test with small amount of batter to test readiness. Dip rattlesnake meat in batter coating thoroughly. Carefully place meat in hot oil to deep fry 3-4 minutes. Turning until rich golden brown in color. Place into warm oven (225 degrees) to hold, no longer than 30 minutes. Top with Avocado Relish in Chapter with Toppers.

DIJON BAR-B-QUED WOODCHUCK

I can not fathom why a woodchuck would be chucking wood to begin with, except to stoke up the Bar-B-Que pit! Woodchucks can reach a sizeable 20 pounds! Most average around 10 pounds, and their meat is dark, but very tender. Woodchucks or "Groundhogs" are a member of the squirrel family and are vegetarians, which is why many hunters say that their meat is so delicious! I prefer to grill or Bar-B-Que this meat, and cook it, as I would tender chicken.

Ingredients:
1 Large Cleaned Woodchuck, Cut into serving pieces
Marinade:
2 Cups Water
1 Cup Apple Cider Vinegar
1 Cup Beer or Ale
1 Cup Onion, Chopped
2 Tbsp. Garlic
1 Tsp. Kosher Salt
1 Tbsp. Black Pepper
Sauce:
½ Cup Onion, Chopped
1 Oz. Bacon Fat
2 Tbsp. Worcestershire Sauce
½ Cup Tomato Paste Thinned with 1/3 Cup Water
2 Tbsp. Apple Cider Vinegar

¼ Cup Lemon Juice
½ Cup Dijon Mustard
2 Cups Wild Game (Venison) Stock
3 Tbsp. Brown Sugar
1 Tsp. Ground Black Pepper
½ Tsp. Kosher Salt
1 Tsp. Garlic Powder
1 Tsp. Onion Powder
1 Tsp. Chili Powder

Preparation: Place cleaned, rinsed and cut Woodchuck meat in a large glass bowl. Remember to remove the glands when cleaning this game animal. Mix all marinade ingredients well and pour over meat. Refrigerate covered for 24 hours. To prepare sauce, first melt fat in large Dutch oven. Add onions and sauté until tender but not brown. Add each remaining ingredient one at a time and slowly to Dutch oven. Heat sauce to boiling; reduce and simmer for 30 minutes until sauce thickens and flavors blend. Remove woodchuck from marinade and pat dry. Place directly on grill over white-hot coals. Grill turning each 5 minutes to different side. In the last 15 minutes add sauce to meat; brushing lightly. Additional sauce may be, reserved for later use. Store remaining sauce in an airtight container in refrigerator.

OVEN BAKED MUSKRAT IN A RED WINE, GARLIC AND BASIL TOMATO SAUCE WITH PENNE PASTA

This recipe is payback for that song by The Captain and Teniel. Muskrats' are said to be the cleanest of all small game animals, and practice very clean habits in the wild. I can say that their meat is very tasty when cleaned and marinated. If you ever have the opportunity to sample this game meat, do so.

Remember that during cleaning to remove the fat layer, scent glands and all of the white tissue located inside of each leg.

Ingredients:
- 1 Large, Cleaned Muskrat
- 2 Cups of Red Wine
- 1 Cup Flour
- 1 Tsp. Kosher Salt
- 1 Tbsp. of Fresh Cracked Black Pepper
- 1 Tsp. Fresh Thyme
- 1 Tsp. Fresh Rosemary
- 3 Tbsp. of Fresh Basil
- 1 Large Onion, Thinly Sliced
- 2 Tbsp. Fresh Minced Garlic
- 8 Tbsp. Olive Oil
- 24 OZ. Tomato Sauce
- 1 Pound of Penne Pasta

Preparation: After cleaning, preparing and cutting the Muskrat (an 8-way cut is preferable) place the meat into a large container. Prepare a soak of two quarts of water, two tablespoons of Kosher salt, and 1 cup of red wine. Cover the game with the soak, cover tightly and place into the refrigerator for 24 hours, turning occasionally. When ready to cook, remove the Muskrat, and drain liquid. In a shallow pan, combine salt and pepper with 1 cup of flour and mix thoroughly. Dredge the meat in the flour, coating evenly. In a large skillet, add 3 tablespoons of olive oil, and slowly heat. Brown the Muskrat lightly and evenly. Remove meat and place into an oven safe baking dish. In the same skillet, add 3 tablespoons of olive oil, onions, garlic and fresh herbs, and lightly sauté. Add the tomato sauce, 1 cup of Red Wine and evenly blend the sauce. Simmer for 30 minutes. Pour sauce over the meat and slow bake in the oven for 1 to 1 & ½ hours until the meat is cooked and tender. An internal temperature of 150 degrees is sufficient. Prepare your pasta in water, ¼ teaspoon of Kosher salt and the remaining 2 tablespoons of olive oil. Cook as desired. Drain the pasta, and plate. Place the finished meat and sauce on top of the pasta and serve. Garnish and serve with fresh grated Parmesan Cheese.

PAN SEARED BEAVER CUTLETS WITH PEPPER MUSHROOM SAUCE

For generations, beaver has been a true American delicacy. Beaver tail remains a true gourmet's delight. Beaver meat is dark, rich and red. Its texture is tender and sumptuous having been compare to roast pork or veal. Young beaver is still preferred for its high quality and grade of game meat. When cleaning, you must remove all fat before attempting to cook. It is recommended to soak the meat in a vinegar solution of 2 quarts cold water, 4 tablespoons of Kosher salt and 2 cups apple cider vinegar. Allow the beaver to soak for 24 hours, then remove rinse in cold water and dry thoroughly.

Ingredients:
6 Beaver cutlet ¾ inch thick
3 Tbsp. Olive Oil
2 Tbsp. Garlic, Chopped
1 Tbsp. Cracked Black Pepper
1 Tsp. Kosher Salt
1 Tsp. Onion Powder
Sauce:
2 Cups Game Stock
2 Cups Red Wine
1 Tbsp. Cracked Black Pepper
1 Cup Mushrooms, Sliced
½ Cup Brown Roux, to thicken

Preparation: Rinse and pat dry the prepared beaver cutlets. Hand rub 1-2 Tablespoons Olive oil on the cutlets. In a large sauté pan, add remaining olive oil and heat on medium until oil is ready. Add garlic and sauté for 1-2 minutes. Add cutlets and sear each side for 1 minute. Lightly season with salt, pepper and onion powder; continue to turn every 2 minutes until cooked to medium. Remove pan from and place in oven to finish cooking until internal temperature is 145 degrees or higher. In a sauce pan stock, wine and pepper on high heat and reduce by 1/3. Add mushrooms add reduce heat to simmer. Slowly whisk in roux to thicken. Plate cutlets and sauce to serve.

SOUTHWEST MESIQUTE BAR-B-QUED JAVALINA

In the Southwest, Javelina or "Peccary", has been considered a Bar-B-Queing wild game favorite for decades. A cousin of the Wild Boar, its savory meat is highly prized. When slow smoked or Pit Grilled, coupled with a long marinade, and sweet Bar-B-Que mop, this small pig provides a dynamic and true Southwestern ethnic flavor.

Ingredients: Hind quarter and ribs of Javelina. Prepare as you would a small suckling pig. Clean and rinse well.

Marinade:
½ Gallon Water
1 Quart Soy Sauce
3 Cups Lime Juice
2 Cups Tequila
1 Garlic, Chopped
1 Cup Pineapple Juice

Preparation: Marinade meat in large plastic bag or container in refrigerator for 24-36 hours. Remove meat and leave wet. Place meat in smoker or on pit that has mesquite chips (soaked 2-3 days in water) on top of white hot coals. Brush with liquid mop (Recipe Honey Bar-B-Que diluted 1 bottle beer) and slow cook, turning meat to insure equal browning. Apply mop with every turn. Cook until internal temperature reaches 145 or higher. Remove Javelina when done, slice and serve with Sweet Pepper & Honey Bar-B-Q sauce.

VENISON AND LARGE GAME

If you gathered all the hunters of venison and large game into one, large hall and asked them one question, what would that question be? I can not give you that answer. I do know what two questions I would not ask. What is the best game to hunt and what game meat tastes the best! With those two questions asked, you might as well pull up a comfortable chair, and have brought your lunch, as it would be a very long debate.

Venison and large game are the heart and soul of game gourmet cooking, this is a fact. During my research for this cookbook, and the compilation of recipes for my soon to be published, second wild game cookbook, "The Buck Stops Here!" I have discovered that wild game cooking, and especially venison cooking has long been a neglected area of the culinary arts.

Wild game recipes seem to fall into two distinct categories. The first category appears to consist of recipes that were created in the 1960's, and embody ingredients and cooking methods that were written from the backs of soup cans and bad hamburger recipes. The second category of game recipes consist of ingredients and methods that were created by a politically correct, frustrated history major, who watches too many cooking show, and "loves to cook for fun and pleasure." Their desire was to "share" (I really hate that word) with the less then enlighten masses their great home discoveries and joys of game foods. If they hunt, then it is probably for sale items at the local junior league shop. Their recipes are lethargically oppressive, with a vast amount of French influence, and the items that are chosen as ingredients must be tracked down with an experienced hunting dog, and a comprehensive list of over priced "specialty stores".

There are very few good, to the point recipes that fall outside of these two categories. When I wrote this cookbook, it was with the purpose of introducing to the general public, (both hunters and non-hunters alike), the fundamental and basic principles of classical cooking for the at home, wild game gourmet. Through simplified techniques and ingredients, most folks will have the opportunity of cooking in an unexplored and neglected culinary wilderness. Without all the unnecessary baggage that normally accompanies most "gourmet" cook books, wild game gourmets may now have a shot at wild game, gourmet cooking. A culinary medium, too long neglected by main stream cooking that deserves closer consideration and well-deserved attention. An area of the culinary arts that does not require a highly refined degree of culinary or cooking experience.

Venison and large game have been combined in this chapter to allow you a condensed guide of different tastes and flavors. I could not possibly have included the vast amount of variations and flavors that venison and large game deserves. That task would have produced a cookbook that would have exceeded a thousand pages or more in length!

This book is a "primer". This is a first step to introduce both the novice and experienced home gourmet, (and those who are not familiar with many complex techniques); a chance to get their feet wet in the forum of simplified game gourmet cooking

Those of you that have dined on venison for years know that venison recipes are propertied to be interchangeable with large game animals. From a chef's point of view, this is not necessarily the case. I believe that all game meats deserve close attention, as each species is different. Wild game and venison recipes have been brutalized by the concept that what ever is good for the deer meat, is good for the moose or elk steak. Let us take venison or deer meat as an example. Venison meat, when it is young and tender, is considered by most game hunters to be the top prize of wild game meats. Venison is dark, very flavorful, and retains a rich exotic flavor. It is not overly wild in taste. With proper preparation and cooking, venison is on a par of good quality prime beef. Unfortunately, most inexperienced wild game cooks have the tendency to poorly prepare and over cook their game meats due in large part to inadequate and improper recipes. Their wild game meats are reduced to a tough and stringy texture. Seasonings and marinades for wild game are often misapplied, and do more harm then good to aiding or preparing the meats for cooking As I have said, venison, large game and wild game is unto itself, unique, and should be regarded that way.

Another area of venison and large game cooking that should be reconsidered is the tendency to reduce venison to repetitive and tired seasonings and flavors. Large game mcats are more suited to exotic seasonings and flavors then most domesticated meats. Elk and Moose are regarded by many to have the honor, (it may be dubious honor) of having the closest flavor to beef. Then why do we season our elk sausage, moose steaks and other large game with flavorings and spices that reduce beef and other domesticated meats to an almost unrecognizable flavor? Branch out and stimulate your wild game meats natural flavors by using any of the hundreds of natural and refined herbs and seasoning that are currently available to the general public. If you are a "meat and tatters" kind of guy, then that is fine. To all the other folks who are tired of the same tastes, I request that your begin to search for new and distinctive flavors and seasoning to try. If you are in search of a place to start, then try my web site. I currently have twelve signature and exotic seasonings on the market!

Wild game meats, venison and large game, (as viewed from this chef's kitchen), has always been a joy to hunt, prepare and serve. If one remembers the few basic principles and procedures when cooking venison and large game, such as proper field and cleaning procedures. Aging, proper marinating and seasoning, larding, and adding fats to your game meats. Most importantly the uniqueness of what we are cooking, I have no doubts that wild game gourmet cooking at home will become more then an art form, practiced by the few.

ROASTED VENISON WITH SHERRY & SAUTEED RED ONION SAUCE

Ingredients:
- 2 Tablespoons Butter
- 3 fresh, large Red Onions, thinly sliced
- 1 Cup Pearl Onions, blanched and peeled
- Kosher salt & fresh ground Black Pepper, (Milled)
- 3 to 4 pound Loin or Roast of Venison
- ½ cup Cooking Sherry
- 2 tablespoons Parsley, fresh, chopped
- 2 tablespoons beef or vegetable base
- 2 cups white wine

Preparation: Combine water, white wine & base together, whisk until blended, and pour the marinade over venison to marinade over night to blunt the game flavor. Before cooking, remove venison, and discard marinade. Sauté sliced Red onions in butter until translucent. Add pearl onions and cook until all onions are soft, at low heat, about 45 minutes. Season lightly with salt & pepper. Rub roast or loin with Kosher salt & pepper, then roast at 325 for about 2 1/2 hour or until the outside of the meat is browned and the internal temperature registers 150 degrees. Remove roast and let stand for 15 minutes. Skim any fats and juices from the roasting pan, place in skillet, add sherry and bring to a boil. Add the onions and parsley, add a dash of pepper, and reduce heat until sauce thickens. Thinly slice the venison, and serve with the onions and sherry sauce.

GRILLED SMOKED VENISON CHOPS WITH JALAPENO BEURRE BLANC SAUCE

This recipe is a blend of the Southwest, and Upper West Side. I have combined two tastes that not only are a key in the most exclusive of eateries, but also have simplified it so that you can prepare this dish at home. I will not mention at what restaurant that I tried this dish, but it was selling at $22.50 a plate!

Ingredients: Four, 6 to 8 Oz Fresh Double Venison Chops
2 Tbsp. Mesquite Flavored Liquid Smoke
2 Tbsp. Olive Oil
Dry Rub Seasonings
1 Tbsp. Kosher Salt
1 Tbsp. Fresh Cracked Black Pepper
1 Tbsp. Chile Powder
1 Tbsp. Garlic Powder
1 Tsp. Cumin
1 Small, Fresh Jalapeno Pepper, De-seeded
Ingredients For the Sauce:
1 Jalapeno Peppers
2 Cups Dry White Wine
½ Cup White Wine Vinegar or Champagne Vinegar
1 Pound of Unsalted Butter, cut into small ½ inch cubes
½ Tsp. White Pepper
½ Tsp. Kosher Salt

Preparation: Pre split the venison chops and rinse. Lightly pat dry the venison chops, and place on a cutting board. Combine the olive oil and liquid smoke and brush the chops evenly. Place on a plate, cover and refrigerate for 1 to 2 hours.

Remove the Jalapeno Pepper stem, and roast the pepper over a burner on high heat until the pepper is blackened and tender. A small pair of tongs works well for this procedure. When pepper is cool, peel, and puree the pepper into a fine paste. Combine with the rest of the rub seasonings, remove the venison and rub them with the pepper rub. Pre heat your grill or broiler. The chops should be grilled over medium coals, broiled at a medium high setting. The chops should be cooked until medium rare to medium. Roast the second Jalapeno pepper; reduce to a finely chopped consistency. Add the Jalapeno pepper into a saucepan, with the wine and vinegar, and on medium high heat reduce by ¾. When liquid is reduced, add the butter cubes, and begin to blend into the mixture until the sauce thickens. Season with salt and white pepper to taste. Serve sauce over the grilled venison chops.

TEXAS STYLE VENISON FAJITAS

There is no other way to enjoy venison flank steak the by creating a "big pile" of Venison Fajitas, with all the trimmings. Fajitas are usually prepared with beef flank steak. If you want to produce the perfect Fajita, the cook the meat too rare, and cut the meat into two-inch strips, ¼ inch wide. The key to a great Fajita is the marinade. Keep it simple, and when you grill the meat, you want to sear it, to lock in the flavors and juices. I recommend that you serve them on a flat iron skillet to re-sear the meat. You can keep the meat warm in the oven as long as there is plenty of liquid on the meat, and it remains covered.

Ingredients: 3 to 5 pounds of Fresh Venison Flank Steak
2 Large Onions
2 Green Bell Peppers, De-seeded
2 Red Bell Peppers, De-seeded
Venison Fajita Marinade
3 Cups Water

2 Cups Soy Sauce
2 Cups Fresh Lime Juice
½ Cup Fresh Lemon Juice
1 Cup of Tequila
1 Tbsp. of Garlic Powder

Preparation: Combine all the marinade ingredients with a whisk. Place venison flank steak into a large bowl and pour the marinade over the meat. Ensure that the meat is evenly soaked. Cover and place into your refrigerator for 24 hours, turning the meat to guarantee even marinating. Slice onions and peppers, and sauté with the butter until soft and tender, place aside and keep warm. Heat your grill to medium high, remove the meat and sear on each side for one minute. The continue to cook meat until cooked to medium. Remove meat, cut, and when serving, place 1 pound of meat onto a very hot flat iron fajita griddle. Top Fajitas with sautéed peppers and onions, and squeeze the juice of ½ fresh lime over the top! Serve this dish with sour cream, grated jack cheese, and fresh Avocado Relish (recipe in Chapter with Toppers) and it is a meal that is beyond compare!

ROASTED LOIN OF VENISON WITH ROSEMARY AND THYME

A traditional dish of roast venison, with the subtle blending of rosemary and thyme. If you enjoy the full flavor of venison, I recommend that if you marinade this meat, you should do it lightly. I prefer to rub the meat with some red wine, verses a marinade. Allow the full and natural flavors to blend and produce their own palate pleasing taste. I also recommend this dish be served with a light Rosemary, or herb sauce, as not to detract from the meat.

Ingredients: 1 Fresh Venison Loin Roast
½ Pound of Bacon, cut into 2 inch slices for

larding the roast
2 Cups of Red Wine
1 Cup Onion, Finely Chopped
1 Tbsp. Garlic, Finely Chopped
1 Tbsp. Fresh Parsley, Finely Chopped
1 Bay Leaf, Crushed
2 Tbsp. Fresh Rosemary, Chopped
2 Tbsp. Fresh Thyme, Chopped
1 Tbsp. Fresh Cracked Black Pepper
1 Tsp. Kosher Salt

Preparation: Take the roast and make your larding cuts in the meat. Rub the roast with the red wine, and let stand for 12 to 24 hours, covered in the refrigerator. In a bowl, combine all remaining ingredients and allow to stand for at least 2 hours. Remove roast and place into a large covered roasting pan. Hand rub the seasoned herb mixture over the roast, cover and place into a preheated, 325-degree oven and slow roast for at least 3 hours, or until meat is medium rare. Remove roast when at desired texture, slice and serve with desired sauce.

SLOW SMOKED VENISON BRISKET WITH HONEY BAR-B-QUE SAUCE

This recipe is another fine regional variation of a Southern treat. Smoked brisket is a wonder to behold. The key to the perfect brisket is to retain as much of a fat layer as possible, and to slow smoke the meat. The ideal procedure is to cook the meat in the smoker at 175 degrees, for 12 to 18 hours, depending on the weight. Since venison should not be over cooked, I would reduce the cooking time by half, to 2/3, and frequently check the meat for doneness. Juicy and rare is the best way to serve brisket.

Ingredients: 1 Large Venison Brisket
¼ Cup Liquid Smoke of Choice

1 Quart Water
2 Tbsp. Vinegar
½ to One Pound of Bacon
1 Tbsp. Fresh Cracked Black Pepper
1 Tbsp. Kosher Salt
1 Tbsp. Garlic Powder
1 Tbsp. Onion Powder
1 Tbsp. Paprika

Preparation: Place the brisket into a large covered roasting pan. Make small even cuts in the brisket, and lard evenly with bacon. I would suggest adding additional bacon sufficient to cover the top of the brisket. Combine the water, liquid smoke and vinegar together, and pour over the meat, and allow to marinate for 24 hours. Combine the spices into a bowl and blend evenly. Remove the brisket and pour off the marinade rub with the seasoned rub, and return to the roasting pan. Place pan into a very low oven, 175-degrees, covered and slow cook for 4 to 6 hours. Check the progress of the meat hourly, and when meat is rare to medium rare, remove and slice (slice across the grain), serve with Honey Bar-B-Que Sauce

GUINNESS MARINADED ELK STEAKS

A fellow chef once told me that there is no such thing as a bad steak, only a badly prepared one! This is true and it applies to Elk in particular. I do so enjoy a large, thick elk steak, prepared with a twist. I use a Guinness Beer soak to give my meat a rich flavor before I put them on the grill. I prefer to soak my steaks in regular Guinness, verses the Guinness Dark Beer or Ale. The richer beers tend to mask the soft game flavor of elk. The choice, I leave up to you, chef!

Ingredients: 4 Large, Fresh Elk Steaks, Cut 1 inch thick
2 – 3 Bottles of Guinness Beer, your choice
Fresh Cracked Black Pepper

Kosher Salt
1 Pound of Fresh Mushrooms, Sliced
2 Large Onions, Sliced
¼ Cup of Butter
½ Cup of Worcestershire Sauce
Steak Butter of Choice

Preparation: Place the Elk steaks into a large, deep pan, and cover them with the Guinness Beer of choice. Allow to marinate from 4 to 24 hours. Before cooking the elk steaks, add the regular butter to a large sauté pan, and heat slowly. Add the onions first, and cook until they soften, then add the mushrooms and sauté together until the mushrooms are tender. Add 1 tablespoon of the Worcestershire sauce, stir and sauté for another 2 minutes, remove or cover, and keep warm. Remove the steaks, and grill over medium high coals, until medium, and fork tender. Lightly brush the steaks with the Worcestershire sauce during each turn of the steaks on the grill. Remove steaks, and serve with steak butter of choice and sautéed mushrooms and onions.

ROASTED ELK WITH A MUSHROOM AND ONION BURGANDY SAUCE

This recipe was designed with the less is better principle of cooking. Keeping this dishes seasonings and preparation as easy and non-complex seems to add to the end result, which is a well flavored, tender roast. I enjoy this dish with a simple Burgundy Wine and Mushroom sauce, which does not detract from the natural flavor of the meat.

Ingredients: 3-4 Pound Fresh Elk Roast
Ingredients for Marinade:
1 Quart Water
2 Cups Burgundy Wine
1/2 Cup Red Wine Vinegar

1 Tbsp. Kosher Salt
1 Tbsp. Fresh Cracked Black Pepper
Seasonings for Elk:
2 Tbsp. Fresh Cracked Black Pepper
1 Tbsp. Kosher Salt
1 Tbsp. Garlic Powder
1 Tbsp. Onion Powder
1 Tbsp. Fresh Dill, Chopped
½ Pound of Bacon, Sliced into 2 inch Cuts
to lard the roast.
1 Large Onion, Sliced
Ingredients for Sauce:
2 Cups Burgundy Wine
2 Cups Fresh Game or Venison Stock
2 Tbsp. Unsalted Butter
2 Cups Mushrooms, Sliced
1 Tbsp. Fresh Cracked Black Pepper
2-3 Tbsp. Cornstarch
Reserved Drippings from the Roasting Pan

Preparation: Combine ingredients for the marinade. Place elk roast into a large container, pour marinade over roast, cover and allow to soak for 12 to 24 hours in the refrigerator. Remove the roast, and make larding cut evenly around roast. Lard the roast with bacon. Blend the spices and herbs, and rub the roast evenly with the seasoning. Place the sliced onions on the bottom of a large covered roasting pan, add a small amount of Burgundy Wine to moisten onions, and place roast into pan and cover. Place roast into a pre-heated, 300-degree oven, and slow roast for 4 hours. Check the roast every hour to ensure meat is not too dry. When the roast is medium rare to medium, remove roast from pan, and hold warm. Remove any onions that are over cooked or blackened. In a saucepan, combine the wine, game stock, pepper and pan drippings and onions, and reduce by 1/3. You may wish to skim the sauce with a spoon to remove any excess fats or grease. In a small sauté pan, add the butter, and mushrooms, and slowly sauté until soft and tender. Add mushrooms to sauce, and allow to simmer for 5 to 10 minutes. Thicken the sauce with a small amount of cornstarch to thicken to desired consistency. Thin slice the roast and serve with the sauce.

GRILLED BUFFALO T-BONE STEAKS WITH GARLIC COMPOUND OR MATER D' BUTTER

Buffalo is one of the un-sung heroes of game gourmet cooking. Although not considered a wild game animal, due to its protected status, commercially raised Buffalo, and the annual monitored Buffalo hunts, this exquisite game meat is readily available year round, from a plethora of sources and outlets. I have encountered people who have tried "Buffalo Burgers" at some roadside stand, and did not like the taste. Most of this meat is a blend of Buffalo, beef, and fats. If you are one of those unlucky customers, this is not the true flavor or taste of Buffalo. Buffalo is what I consider, to represent the truest of American game meats.

Ingredients: 6 Buffalo T-Bone Steaks, 1 inch thick
2 Tbsp. Hunters Spice & Herb Dry Rub (Seasoned Salt)
Maitre d' Butter

Preparation: Rinse and pat dry steaks, rub thoroughly and evenly steaks with spice and herb rub. Broil or grill steaks, 8 minutes on first side turn and continue for an additional 6 minutes for medium doneness. Plat and serve with butter.

TRADITIONAL BUFFALO ROAST

Buffalo Roast has always been a delicacy. When the recipe and seasonings are simple, and the natural flavors of the meat is allowed to peak and remain, Buffalo is a superb choice as a main course wild game meat dish

Indigents: 4-5 Lb. Buffalo Roast
Marinade:
1 Quart Cider, Draft if possible
½ Pint Wine Vinegar
2 Onions, Sliced
2 Carrots, Peeled and Sliced
1 Large Bouquet of herbs
5-6 Whole Black Peppercorns
2 Oz. Gin
1 Bay Leaf
3 Tbsp. Olive Oil
Roast:
½ Pound Bacon, Sliced for Larding
2 Tbsp. Garlic, Minced
2 Tsp. Kosher Salt
2 Tbsp. Cracked Black Pepper
2 Tsp. Garlic Powder
1 Bay Leaf
2 Cloves
1 Cup Orange Juice

Preparation: Rinse and pat dry buffalo roast; place in large container. In a small saucepan, place all ingredients (except oil) of marinade. Simmer on medium for 20 minutes. Remove from heat and cool. After reaching room temperature slowly, whisk in olive oil. Cover roast with mixture and place covered in refrigerator of 24 hours. Turn meat occasionally to evenly disperse marinade. Remove roast from marinade and pat dry. Make small 1 inch incisions in meat and insert bits of bacon and garlic. Rub and thoroughly coating roast with mixture of salt, pepper and garlic powder. In a large Dutch oven, place a small amount of olive oil and heat. Put roast in pan and sear on all sides to lock in juices. Cover with orange juice in which you have placed bay leaf and cloves. Place covered Dutch oven with roast in a preheated 325 degree oven. Baste every 20 minutes and cook 25 minutes per pounds or internal temperature reaches 150 degrees.

RED WINE MARINATED MOOSE ROAST WITH CRACKED BLACK PEPPER SAUCE

Moose is recommended by many sportsman and game meat gourmets as the other "It tastes like Beef" meat. Moose is a very adaptable game meat whose texture, soft game flavor and cooking potential is as good as any domesticated meat. I have to agree that when moose is properly marinated, and is cooked with loving care, it would give prime beef a run for its money! Move over Bossy

Ingredients:
6-7 Lb. Moose Rump Roast
Follow Marinade for Large Game
4 Tbsp. Olive Oil
2 Tbsp. Cracked Black Pepper
2 Tsp. Kosher Salt
2 Tsp. Garlic Powder
1 Large Onion, Sliced
4 Tbsp. Worcestershire Sauce
½ Cup Red Wine
1 ½ Cups Water
Cracked Black Pepper Sauce in Chapter

Preparation: Follow directions for Marinade for Large Game, remove moose roast from marinade pat dry. Rub roast with olive oil, and then sprinkle with pepper, salt and garlic powder. Place sliced onion in bottom of large roaster. Pour 2 tablespoons Worcestershire over onions; place roast on top and pour remaining 2 teaspoons over roast. Add 1 up water and wine to roasting pan. Cover and bake at 325 degrees for 3 ½ to

4 hours; add water or wine as needed to keep moist. Baste occasionally. Internal temperature should be 150 degrees or higher. Remove, carve, plate and serve with Cracked Black Pepper Sauce.

ANTELOPE KABOBS WITH POLYNESSIAN SAUCE and GRILLED VEGETABLES.

Antelope is a very fine choice for wild game meat, gourmets. In recent years, Antelope has not only become a great game to sport hunt, its meat has now, become recognized for its culinary potential. Many "old timers" swore that antelope was as good as venison, but was considered by many as a second choice if venison or elk were available.

Ingredients: 3 Lbs. Antelope steak, cut into 2-inch cubes
3 Cups Buttermilk Marinade (Marinades Chapter)
2 Tbsp. Olive Oil
3 Onions, Medium, cut into chunks
1 Green Bell Pepper, cut into chunks
1 Yellow Bell Pepper, cut into chunks
16 Oz. Can of Chunked Pineapple with juice
1 Tsp. Kosher Salt
1 Tbsp. Cracked Black Pepper
2 Tbsp. Worcestershire Sauce
3-4 Tbsp. Olive Oil
Polynesian Sauce Recipe (Chapter on Sauces)

Preparation: Place cubed steak in covered container and pour over Buttermilk marinade. Marinade in refrigerator 4-6 hours. Remove from marinade and pat dry. In a large sauté pan, heat oil and add Worcestershire sauce; carefully add steak browning on all sides. Remove steak and allow to cool. To saucepan from steak add juice from pineapple, salt and pepper continue to cook for 3-5 minutes; stirring to blend. Retain for basting of kabobs during grilling. Alternate steak, onions, bell peppers and pineapple chunks on skewers. Place on grill over white-hot coals, turning frequently and basting. For medium doneness, process should be 15-20 minutes. Remove from skewers and serve.

SEARED RAM CHOPS WITH LIME & GINGER SAUCE

If ever you receive the opportunity to hunt BigHorn Sheep, Dall or Desert Bighorn, go for it! Mountain Sheep, as they are commonly referred, are by far, another of nature's game gourmet meals waiting to happen. Not only are these beautiful animals one of the most majestic, their meat is of such a tender, rich flavored and flavorful quality (there is a soft mutton under-taste), this game meat is a joy to cook. Remember to remove any fat layer, and prepare as if your were cooking a fine lamb or young venison chop.

Ingredients:
4 Rams Chops, 1 inch thick
16 Oz. Can Chunked Pineapple with liquid
½ Cup Soy Sauce
1 Tbsp. Cracked Black Pepper
1 Tsp. Kosher Salt
½ Tsp. Dry Mustard
2 Tbsp. Olive Oil
¼ Cup Brown Sugar
1 Tsp. Cornstarch
¼ Cup Apple Cider Vinegar
Ginger & Lime Sauce Recipe (Chapter with Sauces)

Preparation: Rinse and pat dry chops; place in covered container. Combine liquid from ½ of pineapple juice, ¼ cup soy sauce, pepper, and salt in a small bowl; pour over chops and refrigerate 4-6 hours. After marinating chops, remove from mixture and pat dry. Over medium high heat in a large skillet add oil; when hot, carefully add chops. Reduce to medium and brown 20 minutes turning every 5 minutes. Add remaining pineapple juice and soy sauce. Reduce heat to low, and cover tightly and continue to cook for 30-45 minutes. Remove chops and hold warm. Mix slowly in cornstarch and brown sugar and heat to boiling. Reduce heat and simmer for 5 minutes to reduce and thicken sauce. Add pineapple chucks and heat thoroughly. Plate chops: pour sauce over and serve.

OVEN ROASTED LEG OF RAM WITH ROSEMARY AND HERB BEARNAISE SAUCE

If you are one of the fortunate few sportsman that have the opportunity to bring home a Ram, then by all means, prepare this recipe. Gently slow roast as you would a leg of lamb. Keep the meat basted and moist with its own stock and juices while cooking. In addition, do not bury this game meat in a sauce. A Béarnaise, of other fine sauce should accompany this dish, not over power it. Keep both the preparation of the game and the sauce subtle and this dish will speak for itself in richness and flavor.

Ingredients:
- 5-6 Lb. Leg of Ram, trimmed
- 2 Tbsp. Rosemary
- 2 Tbsp. Olive Oil
- 2 Tbsp. Basil
- 2 Tbsp. Fresh Cracked Black Pepper
- 1 Tbsp. Kosher Salt
- 1 Tsp. Paprika
- 1 Tbsp. Garlic, Minced
- Herb Béarnaise Sauce recipe (Chapter Sauces)

Preparation: Combine rosemary, pepper, oil, basil and paprika in a small bowl. Wash trimmed and cleaned leg; pat dry. Rub leg with oil mixture; and place in refrigerator for 4-6 hours. Remove and place on rack in roasting pan. Sprinkle with salt. Place in 325-degree oven for 2 ½ hours. Continue to baste with drippings to add moisture. Check meat for desired texture, and internal temperature should reach 145-degrees. Remove and thin slice, and serve with Herb Béarnaise Sauce

BROILED BEAR STEAKS WITH SPICY MUSTARD MARINADE

Bear is a game meat that is either adored or despised. I have found very few sportsmen that will disagree that bear have both a nasty disposition, and if not cleaned, marinated and cooked properly will taste as equally disagreeable! Bear meat, and its unique taste, is directly influenced, by its diet and available food source. Many outdoorsman debate the " hibernation issue", as to when a bear's meat is at its best. I can not answer that question. I will say that it is important too properly cook your bear in excess of 150 degrees, to prevent Trichinosis, which is common in bear meat.

Ingredients: 4 Bear Steaks cut 1 inch thick
3 Tbsp. Olive Oil
Marinade:
1 Cup Red Wine
3 Tbsp. Orange Juice
1 Tbsp. Lemon Juice
2 Green Onions, Chopped
1 Carrot Diced
2 Stalks Celery, Chopped
1 Tsp. Paprika
1 Tsp. Garlic, Minced

1 Tsp. Cracked Black Pepper
1 Tsp. Kosher Salt

Preparation: Rinse and pat dry bear steaks; place in covered container. Combine marinade ingredients in small bowl; pour over steaks and place in refrigerator and marinate for 24 hours. Remove steaks and pat dry. Heat oil in sauté pan over medium high heat; add steaks and sear on both sides, 2 minutes each to lock in moisture. Broil in oven for 5 minutes; turn steaks and broil for 4 more minutes.

HERB SAVORY BEAR STEAKS.

A chef I once met recommended that bear meat is best prepared using a good blend of herds to enhance the flavor of the meat. I had the opportunity to try this dish at his restaurant, and I agree that there is truth to that cooking tip. I do recommend trying a number of herb variations with your bear meat. It appears to aid to the natural flavor, and adds a pleasant undertaste to the dish.

Ingredients: 4 Bear steaks, 1 ½ inches thick, trimmed
1 Onion, Sliced
½ Cup Red Wine
½ Cup Water
½ Cup Vegetable Oil
1 Tbsp. Cracked Black Pepper
1 Tsp. Kosher Salt
1 Tsp. Paprika
1 Tsp. Garlic Powder
1 Bay Leaf

Preparation: Wash bear steaks and pat dry; place in covered container. Mix all remaining ingredients and pour over bear.

Leave covered in refrigerator for 12-24 hours turning meat occasionally. Remove steaks from marinade and pat dry. Heat 4 Tbsp. of olive oil in a large skillet over medium high heat. Brown steaks, turning frequently to avoid sticking. Cook until bear has reached internal temperature of 150 degrees.

GLAZED CARIBOU SHORT RIBS

I had the opportunity to try this game meat a few years ago, and was very pleased with its flavor, and pleasant texture. Caribou is considered by many, a great game animal to hunt. I have not had the opportunity to go after Caribou, but I will attest that their meat is very good, and works well adapting to seasonings and preparation and cooking.

Ingredients:
- 6 Pieces Caribou shortribs, 3-inch lengths
- 3 Tbsp. Flour
- 1 Tsp. Kosher Salt
- ¼ Tsp. Cracked Black Pepper
- ¼ Tsp. Garlic Powder
- ¼ Tsp. Paprika
- 2 Tbsp. Olive Oil
- 1 Onion, Finely Chopped
- ½ Cup Celery, Diced
- 2 Tsp. Dark Brown Sugar
- 1 Cup Sweet White Wine
- ½ Cup Water
- ½ Tsp. Dry Mustard
- ¼ Cup Apple Cider Vinegar
- 2 Tbsp. Worcestershire

Preparation: Rinse and pat dry shortribs. Combine flour, salt, pepper, garlic powder, and paprika in shallow dish. Dredge shortribs in flour mixture insure to evenly coat. Heat oil on medium high in large skillet. Place ribs in skillet browning evenly. Remove to baking dish. Add onions to skillet and sauté until tender. Add celery, sugar, wine, water, dry mustard, vinegar and Worcestershire sauce and heat to a boil. Reduce heat and simmer for 5 minutes. Pour sauce over ribs, cover and place in a 350 degree oven for 1 ½ to 2 hours or until tender.

BOAR CHOPS WITH MUSHROOMS AND PEPPERS

I got the opportunity to hunt boar in Europe. My luck was not with me that day, and I came home without a shot fired. One of the other hunters in our group had better luck, and I will admit that the meat was outstanding. I have also tasted Wild Boar from the United States, and will sing its praises. Boar has a "wild pork-like flavor", but is richer. Like bear the flavor of wild boar meat, is influenced by both diet, and age. If you are fortunate enough to bag a young, well nourished boar, then you will have a true culinary treat to prepare and dine on!

8 Boar Chops
2 Cups Basic Red Burgundy Marinade
3 Tbsp. Olive Oil
½ Cup Red Wine
1 Cup Mushrooms, Sliced
1 Green Bell Pepper, Coarsely Chopped
½ Cup Red Bell Pepper, Coarsely Chopped
½ Cup Yellow Bell Pepper, Coarsely Chopped
1 Tsp. Kosher Salt

1 Tbsp. Cracked Black Pepper
1 Tbsp. Oregano
1 Tbsp. Garlic, Minced

Preparation: Rinse and pat dry boar chops; marinate in covered container in refrigerator for 4-6 hours. Remove form container and pat dry. Heat oil in large sauté pan, carefully add chops and brown evenly on both sides about 6 minutes each or internal temperature reached 150 degrees. Remove and hold warm in oven. Add wine to sauté pan; deglaze by scraping and residue from bottom. Add remaining ingredients and sauté for 5-6 minutes. Remove chops from oven, plate and top with vegetable mixture to serve.

WHISKEY SOAKED SADDLE OF BOAR

This is my favorite recipe for boar. There is nothing better then bourbon soaked wild boar. I am a fan of Jack Daniel's Whiskey. I have cooked with whiskeys and liquors for years, and when used correctly, can accent a dish as no other component can. Try this dish if you like the flavor of wild boar, and try the whiskey too!

Ingredients: 3-4 Lb. Saddle of young boar
2 Cups Sippin Whiskey Marinade
3 Tbsp. Lemon Juice
2 Tbsp. Olive Oil
3 Tbsp. Garlic, Crushed
1 Tsp. Thyme
Tsp. Cracked Black Pepper
½ Cup Water
2 Oz. Jack Daniel's or other whiskey
Bourbon Whiskey Sauce (Sauce Chapter)

Preparation: Place rinsed and patted dry saddle in marinade and cover in container; allow to marinade in refrigerator overnight. Remove saddle and pat dry. Blend lemon juice, oil, garlic, thyme and pepper and run into saddle. Place in roasting pan; add water and cook uncovered in a 325 degree oven for 1 ½ to 2 hours or internal temperature reaches 145 degrees, basting frequently with pan drippings. Remove from oven and remove saddle from pan. Place pan on stove over medium heat; add Jack Daniel's to deglaze, scrapping residue. Reduce by 1/3, do not boil. Slice saddle into serving pieces; plate and pour sauce over to serve.

FISH & AND OTHER THINGS THAT SWIM

Fish as compared to other meats is by nature's devise, much simpler to prepare, clean and cook. There are by comparison to other meats, a few basic and simple knife cuts to perform. There are hundreds of different types of fish to select from, (both freshwater, and seafood variety) yet all are cleaned, cut of filleted virtually the same. Land animals are fewer in number, but require a vastly greater number of cuts and trims to produce an endless array of chops, ribs steaks and roasts!

As compared to land game animals, and fowl, fish possesses very little connective tissue, and tendons and ligament attachments. Fish, is naturally tender. If prepared properly, fish will never be tough in texture. If you overcook, or attempt to "fast cook" a fish, then the results will be a tough texture to the fish. High cooking temperatures effect the proteins of the meat, and cause it to toughen.

Fish will cook very quickly. If you fry, poach, or bake fish, the cooking times should be monitored closely for the best cooking results. Individual recipes and tastes differ greatly. I have been asked many times as to the best way to prepare a fish, or a seafood dish. My answer has always been that the best way to prepare a fish is to the liking of the person that I am serving it to!

I enjoy most fish and seafood, prepared in a variety of ways. I have encountered folks during my travels that would not touch a poached fish for any price! Therefore, I shall present to you the textbook answer on fish preparation. The preferred method of preparing a fish for the most tender and tastiest results is to employ a "moist heat, or poaching method". This method of cooking ensures that the fish retains the greatest amount of fluids, liquids and juices both on and in the tissue, and during the cooking process.

Poaching and other moist heat cooking procedures not only allow you a greater variety of flavor options, but also shall almost guarantee the moistest and tender results. Pan searing, frying, and battering and deep frying fish provides a " stable coating, or shell" that works on the similar principle of locking in moisture into the fish's tissue. This artificial "tissue stabilizer" provides a firmer coating to both hold the fish tissue together, and allowing the fish to cook throughout. Poached fish will, as we have experienced, fall apart, of flake apart very easily when prepared. Care is needed to ensure that fish is not overcooked, regardless of what method is employed.

How can one tell when fish is not over cooked. There are several simple examples, which are tried and true as to whether your fish is not over cooked. If the fish "simply separates or flakes", that is to say that the fish tissue flakes, but does not fall apart easily, then the fish is not over cooked. If there is bone present in the cut of fish, and the tissue separates from the bone easily, and the bone shows no distinct pink coloration, then your fish is fine. The most obvious method is to observe the color of the tissue itself. Fish, when cooked, shall usually have a rich, white or translucent color, (depending on the type of fish). These are the three simplest checks to perform as to the doneness of your fish.

Another point to preparing fish is to determine if your fish is a lean or fat fish. Certain types of fish possess a higher degree of fat then others. As for example cod, sole, bass, snapper, perch and pike are considered "lean" fish. Trout, salmon, tuna and mackerel are considered "fat" fish.

When cooking lean fish, remember that a leaner type of fish will cook dryer, and is normally served with a sauce to add some moisture back into the dish. A few suggestions on methods for cooking a leaner fish are to use a moist or poaching method. Another suggestion is to bake or broil your fish, and frequently baste the fish with a liquid or butter. A third recommendation for leaner fish when fried or pan sautéed is to introduce a "fat" such as butter, oil, or a small touch of liquid to both flavor and assist with the cooking process.

When preparing a fish with a higher fat content, poaching works equally as well for cooking. Fish with a higher fat content tends to cook much better when baked or broiled, requiring less butter or fat to be introduced to the cooking process. Another benefit is that some of the fats and oils are eliminated by this dry heat method. When frying or sautéing a fish with a higher fat content, you do not have to add a large degree of fats to the cooking process. It is recommended that when frying a fattier fish, that you drain or remove as much excess oil and fat when the fish is finished cooking. The "paper towel method" will work fine for this purpose.

When asked what suggestions I have on cutting fish, I can only recommend that it should be left up to the individual as to how he or she prefers their fish cut. I have never had a firm opinion as to what cut is better. I prepare and cut my fish according to the requirements and structure of the particular recipe that I am preparing at the time. If a recipe requires that I prepare a fish whole, then I do so. If you prefer to only dine on fillet cuts, then by all means, enjoy!

Fish will deteriorate very quickly. Fish is considerably, the most fragile of all meats or game. I suggest that when taking game fish, that you should keep them fresh and stable, or alive as long as possible. When you are in a position or place to do so, clean your fish and pack it on ice immediately. When cleaning and preparing fish, use this health and safety rule of thumb.

Fish, either fresh or salt water or seafood, are considered the most potential, and greatest risk to the person handling them, for bacterial contamination. Fish live in a perfect bacterial medium, and can cause a nasty infection or illness if not properly cooked or handled. Always have some form of anti-bacterial soap on hand. Secondly, if cut or "stick" or injure yourself on a fin or barb, clean the wound immediately! I never handle any seafood or fish, either professionally or at home without a pair of latex gloves. I learned the hard way during my youth, as to how quickly one can gain an infection from fish or seafood. The lesson was learned!

There is one final point that I would like to impress on you at home, game gourmets. When cooking fish, it is always recommended to check the internal temperature of your cooked fish. I personally check or monitor the temperature of fish, and will not eat it unless it has an internal temperature of 165 degrees or higher. At this temperature, I am fairly confident that most, if not all potentially harmful bacteria are dead. Always wash and clean your work area well, and never store raw fish (or any raw meats of fowl) where they may leak onto any other foods. Common sense is a must, when handling and preparing fish, and other things that swim.

LEMON BAKED FISH

This recipe may be applied to most, if not all fish. I recommend that you zest your dish with fresh dill, lemon or other combinations of tangy citrus items to add a wilder and tangy flavor to this dish!

Ingredients: 6pcs. 8 oz. of fish fillets
1 Tsp. Kosher Salt
1 Tbsp. Fresh Cracked Black Pepper
1/3 Cup Lemon Juice
1 Tsp. Paprika
½ Cup Onions, Chopped
4 Tbsp. Butter
1/3 Cup Parsley, Chopped
½ Cup Green Onions, Chopped, Tops and Bottoms
1 Tbsp. Vegetable Oil

Preparation: Combined lemon juice, salt, pepper and paprika in small bowl and whisk. Dip each fillet into mixture. Place in a lightly oiled baking dish (1 tbsp. vegetable oil) and cover and refrigerate for one hour. Lightly sauté onion in butter until tender and soft. Place aside and keep warm. Take fish form refrigerator cover pan with foil. Bake fish at 400° for about 10 minutes or until fish reaches internal temperature of 165. When fish is at proper temperature remove foil. Top each portion with a spoonful of onion and parsley mixture. Place back in oven and back for an additional 5 minutes. Remove fish, plate and garnish with Lemon wedges and fresh parsley.

PAN FRIED PIKE or Other Game Fish

There are few pleasures know to anyone, except to sport fishermen, and outdoorsmen, then the smell of fresh, pan fried fish, beside a warm campfire, under a cool blue morning sky. I am not, by any stretch of the imagination, a great outdoorsman. Every blue moon, I strike out for the rivers and the woods, and practice a great escape from the modern world. This recipe allows me to "escape" whenever I prepare it!

Ingredients: 6 pcs. 8 oz. Fillets
1 Cup Cornmeal
1 Cup Flour
1Tbsp. Kosher Salt
1 Tbsp. Fresh Cracked Black Pepper
1 Tbsp. Garlic Powder
1 Tbsp. Onion Powder
1 Tbsp. Paprika
3 Large Eggs, Beaten
1 ½ Cup Whole Milk
¼ Cup Lemon Juice
2 Cups Peanut Oil

Preparation: Soak fish in lemon juice for one hour covered and refrigerated. Blend cornmeal, flour and seasonings. Combine eggs and milk; whisk well to blend. Remove fillets; shake off excess lemon juice. Dip fillets in egg mixture and then roll in flour cornmeal mixture. Heat oil on medium high testing a small piece of breading to make sure oil is ready. Place fillets in oil; brown fillets from 3 to 5 minutes each side until golden brown. Remove fish place on rack on baking sheet. Place in 350 oven to finish baking. Check internal temperature. When it reaches 165, they are ready to serve.

CHEF BIG JOHN'S MISSISSIPPI STYLE BUTTERMILK CATFISH

This recipe is dedicated to a great chef, and a good man. Chef John Roland is a chef that I knew that would produce this outstanding dish. Patrons would drive for miles to sample this recipe, and it soon became an area favorite! Big John, this recipe is yours, and the gratitude and things that you taught me are written here, with thanks!

Ingredients: For the Marinade
1 Quart Buttermilk
1 Tablespoon Black Ground Pepper
1 Teaspoon White Pepper
1 Teaspoon Salt
1 – 1 ½ Tablespoon Tabasco Sauce
4 to 6 8oz Catfish Fillets
3 Cups Cornmeal
1 Cup White Flour
1 Tablespoon Paprika
1 Tablespoon Salt
1 Tablespoon Ground Black Pepper
1 Tablespoon Cayenne Pepper
½ Teaspoon Chili Powder
½ Teaspoon Garlic Powder
Vegetable Oil as needed for frying

Preparation: After filleting and cleaning your catfish, rinse, then soak in cool ice water for ½ hour. Combine Buttermilk, white & black pepper, salt & Tabasco Sauce in a large bowl, and whisk together for 1 minute. The bowl needs to be large enough to soak all the catfish in without overflowing. Remove catfish from water, shaking of the excess water, and place into the Buttermilk marinade for 1 to 3 hours. Cover and place into refrigerator to soak. Combine all other ingredients into a mixing bowl, whisk together, creating an even mix of ingredients, then place into a large dish or pan so you can dredge and pat the fillets. Remove fillets from refrigerator; take 1 fillet and place in cornmeal dredge. Cover fillet with cornmeal dredge and press firmly to impress the mixture with the fillet. If you wish an "extra crispy" style, dip the fillet back into the marinade and repeat the dredging process. Place on a pan until all fillets are ready to fry. In a large skillet, (a seasoned, cast iron skillet is the best) place ½ inch of oil and heat. Test oil by placing a small bit of wet dredge into the pan. If it begins to "deep fry", the oil is ready. Place fillets into pan and cook until color is golden brown. Then remove fillets from skillet, place on wire rack, to drain excess oil. When all fillets are done, place wire rack onto a sheet pan, and place into a 350° degree oven to finish baking. Test for done with a thermometer. Internal temperature should be 165 degrees or better. Remove and serve.

TROUT ALMANDINE A LA GRILL

This recipe was created at a resort that I worked at a number of years ago. This was one of our house specials, and was well received by our customers. I was amazed at how flavorful and adaptive trout was to this combination of ingredients. It is simple, yet when presented correctly, will serve as a true gourmet dish.

Ingredients:
- 6 Fillets of Trout (8 oz)
- 2 Eggs
- 1 Cup Milk
- Flour
- 2 Cups Vegetable Oil
- 1 lb. Almonds, finely chopped
- 1 Cup Butter
- 1 Lemon
- 1 Tbsp. Parsley, Chopped
- 1 tsp. Worcestershire sauce
- Salt and Pepper to taste

Preparation: Season Trout with salt and pepper and roll in flour. Beat eggs into milk, then dip fillets into mixture. Fry slowly in oil until golden brown. Remove fish from skillet and cover with crushed or chopped almonds. Brown butter until golden brown and remove from heat. Squeeze lemon into butter and add Worcestershire sauce and parsley, pour over fish and serve.

BAKED STUFFED FISH

This is a versatile recipe that may be applied to about any type of game fish. I have always enjoyed stuffed fish dishes, and am sure that this will also become one of your favorites.

Ingredients: 8 pcs. 8 oz. Fillets
3 Cups prepared stuffing (Sides Chapter)
1 Cup Canned or Whole Milk
1 Cup Onions, Sliced
Salt and Pepper to taste

Preparation: Stuff each fillet with ½ cup of stuffing. Sprinkle with salt and pepper. Pour milk in bottom of roasting pan. Place fish on top. Top with sliced onions. Bake at 350° for 45-50 minutes. Remove with spatula and serve warm.

CAJUN FRIED FISH

If you enjoy and crave a hot and wild fish creation, then this recipe should hit the spot. I cannot pull myself away form Southern Cuisine. It has a degree of life and spirit that is rarely found in other regional cuisines. Fishing has been compared to "an additional or comparative religion" in the south. It requires study, patience, a lot of faith, and an occasional immersion or baptism in the water. I love the South, and good southern game fish recipes!

Ingredients: 6 pcs. 8 oz. Fillets
2 Cups Cornmeal
¼ Cup Water
¼ Cup Non-light Beer
¼ cup Hot Sauce or Tabasco Sauce
½ tsp. Fresh Cracked Black Pepper
½ tsp. Kosher salt
½ Tsp. Chili Powder
½ Tsp. Garlic Salt
½ Tsp. Onion Powder
½ Tsp. Cayenne Pepper
2 Cups Vegetable Oil

Preparation: Soak fillets in water, beer and hot sauce for 4 hours covered in refrigerator. Combine cornmeal and spices; blend evenly together. Remove fillcts from marinade, shaking excess and roll in cornmeal mixture. When well breaded, place aside. Heat oil on medium high temperature; test with small piece of breading to assure oil is ready. Carefully add fillets; fry 3-5 minutes each side or until brown. Remove fillets; drain excess oil.

BLACKENED FISH WITH CREOLE SAUCE

Louisiana and New Orleans in particular are renowned for the ability to draw the best seasonings and flavors from a lowly fish. My wife and I would find excuses to take a Louisiana road trip, just to have a great meal, a few tall Hurricanes at Pat O'Briens on Bourbon Street. We would shop the markets and venders to stock up on fresh seafood and spices. We would always have a cooler or two of fresh goodies to return home with, and the drive would always hurry by as we planned our next "necessary trip" to New Orleans.

Ingredients: 2-3 lbs. Fish Fillets ½ inch thick
4 Tbsp. Butter, Add more if needed.
2 Tbsp. Paprika
2 Tbsp. Garlic Power
2 Tbsp. Red Pepper
2 Tbsp. Kosher Salt
1 ¼ Tsp. Pepper, White
1 ¼ Tsp. Cracked Black Pepper
1 ½ Tsp. Thyme Leave
1 ½ Tsp. Oregano

Preparation: Rinse fillets in cool water. In a mixing bowl blend together herbs and spices evenly. Melt butter in a small shallow baking dish. Dredge and fully coat fillets in butter. Coat thoroughly in dry mixture, pressing into fish until evenly coated. Preheat dry cast iron skillet on medium high. When skillet has reached temperature a drop of water should bead and roll. Place fillets in hot skillet. Cook for 3-5 minutes each side until a blackened coating has fully formed. Remove from pan place on rack baking sheet. Place in 350 oven to finish until internal temperature reached 165. Remove and serve with Creole sauce.

TRADITIONAL ALLIGATOR STEW

If you have the opportunity to purchase some fresh alligator, then do so. The tail meat is as fine as any game meat you would desire. It is a fact that alligator is an acquired taste, but once you have tried it, you will find yourself coming back for more. If nothing else, you can tell your friends that you tried a dish that had quite a bite, and had the opportunity to bite back!

Ingredients:
5 Pounds Fresh Alligator Tail Meat
3 Stalks Celery
2 Stalks Chopped Green Onion
1 Green Bell Pepper
1 Red Bell Pepper
16 Oz of Tomato Paste
1 Tablespoon of Cayenne Pepper
1 Tablespoon Cracked Black Pepper
1 Tablespoon of Kosher Salt
2 Tablespoons of Minced Garlic
¼ Cup Chopped Onion
1 Bay Leaf, Whole
6 Quarts of Water
1 Quart of Red Wine
1 Quart of Shrimp stock

Preparation: Rinse, clean, and cube into ½ inch cubes five pounds of fresh alligator tail meat. Sauté vegetables. Mix 1 & ½ gallons of cool water, 1 quart of red wine, and 1 quart of shrimp or seafood stock into a large stockpot. Bring to a rapid boil. Add the tomato paste, add the vegetables, and reduce slowly for 1 to 2 hours. Sauté the alligator meat in a large sauté pan, lightly browning, (flour, salt, and pepper). Add meat to stockpot and simmer for 2 to 3 hours, stirring to prevent sticking. When meat is tender, you may serve. Recommend serving over dirty rice.

GRILLED ALLIGATOR TAIL STEAKS.

I was at a Bar-B-Que in Louisiana once in which a Cajun friend of mind had invited me to. He said it was a family get-together, and upon arrival, I discovered that I was there with about 300 people. I asked if these folks were all his kin. His answer was, "CY down here, we is all related to somebody"!

Ingredients
6-1 Inch Thick Alligator Tail Steaks
Ingredients for Marinade:
2 Bottles of Non-Light Beer
½ Cup Fresh Lemon Juice
2 Cups White Wine
¼ Cup Hot Sauce or Tabasco Sauce
2 Cups Water
2 Tablespoons Fresh Cracked Black Pepper
1 Tablespoon Kosher Salt
2 Tablespoons Chile Powder
¼ Cup Fresh Minced Garlic
Ingredients for "Mop":
3 Tablespoons of Liquid Smoke
½ Cup Non-Light Beer
½ Cup White Wine
1 Tablespoon Fresh Cracked Black Pepper
1 Teaspoon of Kosher Salt
1 Tablespoon Garlic Powder
1 Tablespoon Onion Powder
1 Tablespoon Cayenne Pepper
1 Tablespoon Chili Powder
1 Teaspoon Paprika

Preparation: Combine all ingredients for the marinade into a mixing bowl and whisk for one minute until thoroughly blended. Rinse and pat dry alligator steaks, place into a large bowl, and add the marinade. Soak the steaks for 12 hours, covered, in a refrigerator. Prepare the mop, by mixing all ingredients, and refrigerate until ready to grill. Heat coals until white hot. Remove steaks from marinade, and quick sear (for 1 minute) steaks on each side to seal in moisture. Using a small brush, begin to "mop" the alligator steaks and turn every 3 minutes on the grill. Cooking times may vary, due to individual grill. Internal temperature should reach 145 degrees for medium. Recommended to be served with Dirty Rice, and hot sauce.

FROGS LEGS SCAMPI STYLE

I first learned to prepare this dish many years ago in Germany. I always enjoyed the blending of flavors and the way that the cooking process promoted a smooth blending of flavors. I wrote this recipe in my first recipe journal and have kept it ever since. It is so good that my 8-year-old daughter will request it about once a month. I can guarantee that it is a promised winner as a grand appetizer, or addition to any seafood or game fish meal.

Ingredients:
- 6 Pair of Fresh Frogs Legs
- 1 teaspoon of Kosher Salt
- 1 teaspoon Cracked Black Pepper
- 2 Tablespoons Fresh Minced Garlic
- 2 Tablespoons of Unsalted Butter
- ¼ Cup of White Wine

Preparation: Clean and rinse frogs legs. Melt butter in large skillet and sauté the garlic for 2 to 3 minutes. Add the frog's legs and brown slowly on medium heat for 5 minutes, turning the frog's legs to ensure even cooking. Add the white wine and continue to cook until wine is reduced by half. Remove from heat, add salt and pepper, and finish baking in the oven until meat is tender and cooked. Remove and serve with sauce form sauté pan. Add lemon and garlic compound butter and serve.

GRILLED SMOKED FROG LEGS

If you have a small smoker of grill, then you will enjoy this variation on a tradition Southern frogs legs recipe. In some parts of the deep south, if it swims, paddles, jumps or dives, then it is fair game. I knew a kid back home who loved nothing more then “giggin frogs”. He was quite adept at catching and securing snapping turtles as well. What his mother never knew was that he would raid her kitchen and use her good knives to clean and skin his catch of the day!

Ingredients: 6-8 Pair of Frog legs
1 Tbsp. Liquid Smoke
1 Tsp. Hot Sauce
¼ Cup Butter
½ Cup Water
½ Cup Lemon Juice
3 Tbsp. Seasoned Salt, use seasoned salt in Chapter VI

Preparation: Clean and rinse frogs legs and place in container. Cover legs in ½ of lemon juice and water; set for 1 hour covered in refrigerator. Create mop by combining butter, liquid smoke, hot sauce, 1 Tbsp. seasoned salt and remaining lemon juice. Remove legs from juice and rub with remaining 2 Tbsp. of seasoned salt. Heat charcoals till the are white hot. Place foil over grate and punch holes for ventilation. Place legs on foil and brush up side with butter mixture. Turn and repeat several times. When meat becomes white and pulls away from the bone they are done.

RAINBOW TROUT POACHED IN WHITE WINE AND DILL

Several weeks ago my neighbor rang my doorbell, and presented me with a half dozen of the most glorious, fat Rainbow trout that I have seen in years. The idea of a fresh rainbow trout, soaked in white wine and lightly seasoned with dill sent me form the study, running to the kitchen. After dinner, I returned to the joy of writing this cookbook, with a recipe that is now for you to enjoy.

Ingredients:

4 Rainbow Trout, Cleaned and Filleted
2 Cups White Wine
2 Tbsp. Dill, dried
2 Tbsp. Dill, Fresh, Chopped
1 Tbsp. Fresh Rosemary, Chopped
1 Tbsp. Kosher Salt
1 Tbsp. Cracked Black Pepper

Preparation:

Place trout in large shallow dish. Add wine, dried dill and allow trout to marinade for 2-3 hours covered in refrigerator. Remove fish from marinade and place in clean baking dish. Add 2 cups fresh white wine, fresh dill, rosemary, salt and pepper. Cover and place in 375 degree oven to poach for 20-30 minutes or until meat is tender and done. Remove skin and lift meat from bones in one solid piece. Serve with small cut on dill and rosemary compound butter.

BIRDS ON THE WING AND IN THE OVEN

I have condensed this chapter to include not only upland game birds, but also waterfowl. It was not an easy choice. I wanted to give the novice, and experienced at home game gourmet a small taste of wild waterfowl, and game birds. I could very easily devote (and plan to) several cook books exclusively to the preparation and cooking of waterfowl, small game birds, and the larger variety of game birds.

This chapter is to provide a small sampling of the varied tastes and flavors of the most commonly hunted and purchased birds available to the game bird and waterfowl hunter, as well as the non-hunting, store purchased game.

Upland game birds are superb for sport hunting. They are a challenge to hunt, but reward the shooter with superior tasting meat. I have met a lot of game bird hunters as well as chefs whose top pick or preference of which bird is best, are as varied as the thousands of methods and recipes for preparation. Woodcock, dove, pheasant, Quail, Chukar, Sage Hen, all of these game birds have their champions. Woodcock is considered by many, to be the best tasting. Woodcock fans are followed closely by dove, quail and pheasant aficionados. No matter what your personal favorite is, we can all agree in the culinary pleasure that is achieved when one of natures true gourmet treasures are plated and served!

Aging of game birds is considered essential for producing finely flavored game bird meat. The debate rages as to how long to age game birds. When I was in Europe, many traditional game chefs would allow their game birds to hang for two to three weeks, uncleaned, or until the tail feathers began to fall off! I inquired as to why hang a game bird for so long.

After a week, most Americans would hold a memorial service and bury their bird! The response was that it took that long to produce what is know as a High or Rich" flavor to the meat. Granted, aging does improve and flavor the meat, but as to a preferred or recommended aging, or "hang time" I have found that 6 to 10 days, under very controlled conditions will produce a fine flavoring to the meat. I have known several devoted game bird hunters that purchased a used refrigerator, devoted to the aging of their fresh killed game birds! It allows them to hang and age their kill in a clean, temperature-controlled environment, and to monitor and control the aging process. Freezing is the most popular method of aging your game birds, but there are still a large number of purists that swear by the tried and true method. My recommendation is to try both aging methods. See which method suits you, or your personal tastes, best!

A few points to remember when hunting upland game birds. Practiced game bird hunters make the time to come to the hunt well prepared for cleaning, and transporting their fresh kill. I will always emphasize to any sportsmen, as to importance of safety in handling their fresh kill. You do not want to go the effort of hunting these great birds, only you have the meat ruined due to poor practices in the field. Take the time to properly cool, field clean, and prepare your game for transport. A small amount of preparation and practice, will result in a superior tasting game dish, and reduce the chances of any unfortunate illness due to spoiled meat.

Waterfowl both large and small are both superb to hunt, and to cook. There are, over 140 different types of waterfowl, and seasonal migratory birds available to hunt throughout the continental United States and Canada. A scant dozen or so of these birds usually receive the lions share of attention due to conventional popularity of both hunting and cooking. The most recognized of the birds is the "King of Canada's Sky's" the Canadian Goose. The best know and recognized of all ducks is the Mallard whose rich, fine flavored meat is always subtle in flavor when not buried in a grand or heavy sauce.

Duck and goose should be enjoyed as close to "natural" as possible. The game flavor of both upland game birds, and waterfowl is rarely that strong or objectionable to warrant killing the flavor with an overpowering or strong sauce. I recommend that when saucing your goose or duck, to use the less is more principle. Use a simple sauce or mild combination of herbs and spices to enhance and compliment the natural flavor of the game.

When you marinade your waterfowl, it is always recommended by chefs to soak or marinade any fresh shoot waterfowl for at least 24 hours. This method will usually remove any potential lingering "fish" flavor should your game have dined on any fish prior to being taken. A popular method is to soak your goose or duck in a solution of cold water, light or flavored vinegar and Kosher salt. My recommended proportion is 2 Tablespoons of Kosher salt, 2 Tablespoons of Cider Vinegar mixed with 1 Quart of cool, fresh water. Be sure to prepare enough of this solution to completely cover the birds for 24 hours.

When you remove your waterfowl from this pre-marinade salt and vinegar bath, I recommend that you immediately and thoroughly wash and rinse your waterfowl in cold running water, then dry completely, both inside and out. Then you may place your game into your preferred marinade. Always remember to clean and refrigerate your kill as soon as possible and always practice good and speedy field cleaning methods. Hunters, shooters and sportsmen always stress safety in the use and handling of firearms. Bad safety and carelessness can be fatal. As a chef, I demand the same level of common sense and safety when handling fresh killed and prepared wild game.

Why take the risk when a little preparation and preventive practices will always prevent a potential mishap!

DUTCH OVEN SIMMERED SESAME DUCK WITH SAUCE

A very simple recipe for those who enjoy a touch of the orient for their wild game bird dishes. I am a big fan of Far East cooking, and have enjoyed experimenting with oriental and Chinese variations with my wild game dishes. I hope that you enjoy my efforts!

3 lbs. Duck Breast, Skinless, Diced
1 Cup Scallions, Chopped
1 Cup Green Chilies, Mild, Sliced
¼ Cup Cornstarch
½ Cup Soy Sauce
¼ Cup Wine Vinegar
¼ Cup Sugar
2 Tbsp. Sesame Oil
1 ¼ tsp. Hot Pepper Oil
2 Tbsp. Gingerroot, Minced
2 Tbsp. Garlic, Minced
3 tsp. Black Pepper
½ Cup Peanut Oil
2 Cups Game Bird Stock

Combine scallions, chilies, cornstarch, soy sauce, wine vinegar, sugar, hot pepper oil, sesame oil gingerroot, garlic and black pepper in large bowl. Add duck meat to mixture. Mix well. Cover and chill for 3 hours. Heat peanut oil in preheated 350° Dutch oven. Add duck mixture. Stir-fry for 7-10 minutes. Add fresh game bird stock, or fresh vegetable stock to mixture. Stir and allow mixture to simmer for 3-5 minutes. Cover and simmer for about 5 minute. Serve hot over seasoned rice pilaf or herbed wild rice, accompanied by Sesame Game Sauce found in Sauce Chapter.

STUFFED PHEASANT

Stuffed Pheasant is a traditional dish, for a non-indigenous game bird. Pheasant has always seemed to represent the American game bird hunter. This was the first game bird that I hunted as a boy. The interesting fact is that this American game bird is not a natural inhabitant of the Americas. It was introduced during the 1880's, and is a native bird of China! The recipe that I have included in this chapter, is a very traditional, American recipe.

1 2-3 Lb. Pheasant
4 Slices of Bacon, Thick
½ Cup + 2 Tbsp. Sherry, Dry
3 Tbsp. Flour
¼ Cup Butter, Melted
2 Cups Game Bird Stock
½ Cup Onion, Chopped
½ Cup + 2 Tbsp. Butter
½ Cup Mushrooms, Chopped
1 Cup Water
½ Cup Uncooked Rice
2 Tbsp. Parsley
¼ Tsp. Kosher Salt
¼ Tsp. Fresh Cracked Black Pepper

Sauté onion in 2 tablespoons butter. Add water to onions and bring to a boil. Slowly add rice, stirring. Cover and cook until all liquid is absorbed, 20 minutes. Add mushrooms and parsley. Add salt and pepper. Spoon mixture loosely into cavity of pheasant. Place breast up in roasting pan. Lay bacon slices over breast and legs. Place in preheated oven at 350° for 1½ hours or until tender. Internal temperature of duck and stuffing must reach 165. Baste pheasant as cooking with mixture of sherry and ½ cup melted butter. Reserve 2 tablespoons of drippings from pan. Slowly blend in flour and then stock. Simmer until thickened enough to coat the back of a spoon. Add 2 tablespoons of sherry, blending evenly. Remove pheasant and carve. Add a sweet or light sauce as desired to serve.

ROAST GOOSE OR DUCK

This recipe is the height of simplicity. I have not attempted to "overkill" this dish with a large amount of herbs or spices. I allow the game flavor to speak for its self. I do not marinade this dish in any complex marinade. I do soak the goose or duck for 24 hours in a weak salt/vinegar solution, and add 1 cup of wine to the soak. I then rinse and dry the game before cooking. I would encourage you to try this dish without a sauce, or create a simple fruit compote or chutney to accompany this dish. I have several examples in the chapter on sauces.

1 Goose or Duck
1 Apple, Peeled, cored and chopped
¼ Cup Fresh Celery, Chopped
½ Cup Fresh Onion, Chopped
¼ Cup Raisins
1 Tbsp. Fresh Minced Garlic
1 Bacon Strip
1 Cup Apricot or Pear Compote
½ Cup Fresh Orange Juice

½ Cup Port Wine

Place goose or duck in shallow roasting pan. Rub with salt and pepper. Combine apple, celery, onion, raisins, and garlic. Stuff bird with mixture. Place bacon over cavity. Cook at 500° for 30 minutes. Reduce heat to 350° and continue for an additional 1 ½ hours or until tender. Melt jelly and juice in a small saucepan. Add wine pour and our mixture over bird while cooking.

QUAIL WITH CHERRY SAUCE

My wife is a fine shot. She learned to hunt both dove and quail in West Texas. When schedules permit, she sets forth each fall for a "shopping on the wing" expedition, that usually keeps the freezer well stocked for the winter season.

8 Quail Breasts, Skinned
½ Flour
½ Tsp. Kosher Salt
½ Tbsp. Garlic Powder
½ Tbsp. Paprika
½ Tbsp. Fresh Cracked Black Pepper
½ Tsp. Onion Powder
½ Cup Peanut Oil
1 Lb. Fresh Dark Cherries
1 Cup Port Wine

Combine all ingredients except breast, oil, cherries and port to paper bag. Add breast two at a time and shake until evenly coated. Heat peanut oil to hot. Add breast and sauté until brown. In a separate pan add pitted cherries, port, and simmer for 45 minutes in low heat. Place breast in shallow pan to finish in oven. Heat in preheated oven at 325° for 25-30 minutes. Remove and place on serving dish. Spoon cherry port sauce over top.

GAME BIRD WITH ONION, BACON AND MUSHROOMS

Another simple recipe that allows the flavors of the game birds to come thru. I enjoy the combination of flavors in this recipe. This dish has always been a fall hunting favorite of mine, as well as game bird hunting friends.

4 Small Game Birds
3 Cups Pearl Onions, Peeled
4 Bacon Slices, Diced
1 1/3 Cups Dry White Wine
2/3 Cup Game Bird Stock
1 Lb. Small Button Mushrooms, Sliced
1 1/3 Cups Heavy Cream
1 Tbsp. Kosher Salt
1 Tbsp. Fresh Cracked Black Pepper
4 Sprigs Fresh Tarragon
8 Tbsp. Butter

In a large sauté pan melt butter over medium high heat until butter is melted and foamy. Add birds and brown 2 minutes each side. Remove birds from pan and set aside. Add onion and bacon to pan, slowly sautéing until golden brown. Slowly add wine and stock to pan. Add birds back into pan. Cover and bake in 350° preheated oven for 30-40 minutes. Add mushrooms and continue to bake covered for an additional 15 minutes. Remove birds and place on serving platter. Heat sauce from baking on very high heat to reduce. Add cream and continue to boil stirring constantly to prevent sticking. Thicken for 10 minutes until thicken. Pour over birds and serve. Garish with fresh tarragon.

SAUTED PHEASANT WITH RED WINE CREAM SAUCE

I first prepared this dish as a special dinner when I was dating my loving wife. I wanted to surprise her with a special, candle light dinner, and show off as to my culinary skills with wild game. It must have worked. We were married within a year. My wife is also an exceptional at home, gourmet cook in her own right. A truly perfect match!

2 Young Pheasants 2 ½ lbs. Each, Quartered
2 Cups Heavy Cream
1 Cup Red Wine
¼ Cup Game Bird Stock
1 Lb. Mushrooms, Medium, Sliced
1 Tsp. Kosher Salt
1 Tbsp. Fresh Cracked Black Pepper
½ Tsp. Garlic Powder
4 Tbsp. Unsalted Butter

Melt 2 tablespoons of butter in a large sauté pan. Large enough to hold the pheasants. Add pheasants to pan and sauté on medium high heat 3-4 minutes on each side, lightly browning. Reduce to low heat and add wine. Cooking for an additional 10 minutes on each side. Remove pheasant from pan and place in baking dish to finish in oven. Bake uncovered at 325° for 10-15 minutes. Add cream, stock, and seasonings to sauté pan with juices. Cook on high heat whisking briskly until thickened. When thicken reduce heat to low simmer. In a small separate sauté pan, add remaining butter and sliced mushrooms, sautéing quickly until tender. Remove pheasants from oven and arrange on serving dish. Pour cream sauce over pheasant. Garnish with mushrooms and serve.

CLASSIC BRAISED DUCK

Duck is best prepared when, either, slow roasted or braised. The rule of thumb from most chefs is to have the duck crispy on the outside, or skin, and have a juicy and tender meat texture. When I cook duck, I tend to pay close attention to the cooking process. This extra attention and care always provides outstanding results!

1 Duckling, about 3 lbs.
4 Tbsp. Butter
2/3 cup Sweet White Wine
2 Cups Game Bird Stock
1 lb. Small Red Potatoes, Halved
1 Small Red Onion, Sliced
1 Red Bell Pepper, Sliced
1 Cup Pearl Onions
1 Tsp. Kosher Salt
1 Tbsp. Fresh Cracked Black Pepper
2 Tbsp. Fresh Parsley, Chopped
1/8 Tsp. Sugar

Melt butter over medium heat. Add duck quarters and brown evenly, about 2 minutes each side. Pour off fat into second pan. Increase pan with duck to medium high heat; add white wine and game stock to duck. Bring to rapid boil. Cover then place in oven at 350° for 30 minutes. Add butter to pan with duck fat. Then add onion, potatoes and bell pepper for sautéing 4-6 minutes over medium heat. Stir in salt, pepper, sugar and parsley. Continue to heat for 5 minutes. Pour over duck and continue to bake covered in oven for an additional 45-50 minutes. Remove duck and vegetables from oven place on serving platter and keep warm. Take juice from baking dish place in sauté pan on medium high heat to reduce and thicken. When thickened pour over duck and vegetables and serve.

ROSEMARY BRAISED QUAIL

Certain flavor combinations seem to work with certain game. I have discovered that rosemary is superb for quail, woodcock, and dove. It does not overpower the game flavor, and has the tendency to blend with the natural flavors of the meat. This is another of my favorites.

8 Quail, whole, dressed and clean
6 Tbsp. Butter
1 Large, Onion, Sliced
2 Cups Celery, Thinly Sliced
½ Lb. Carrots, Sliced
2 1/3 Cups Fresh Game Bird Stock
½ Cup Dry White Wine
1 Tsp. Kosher Salt
1 Tbsp. Fresh Cracked Black Pepper
2 Tbsp. Fresh Rosemary, Chopped
½ Red Bell Pepper, Sliced
1/3 Cup Green Onion Tops (Chives)

Melt 2 tablespoons butter over medium heat. Add julienne vegetables and lightly sauté for 5 minutes; then set aside. In a large sauté pan, add remaining 4 tablespoons of butter. Over medium heat place quail and sauté for 5 minutes turning once. Add stock and wine to birds simmer for 10-15 minutes. Place vegetables on warming dish. Nest quail in vegetables and hold warm in oven. Add rosemary, salt and pepper. Reduce by 1/3 over medium high heat; allow sauce to thicken to medium consistency. Pull birds from oven; pour reduced sauce over birds, garnish and serve.

CAJUN STYLE WHOLE FRIED TURKEY

If you have never had the opportunity to try this truly regional taste treat, then you are missing out on one of the South's best contributions to American holiday dining. In Texas, a group of friends would pitch in to purchase a freestanding gas-fired "pot fryer" and have a turkey frying party on a Saturday afternoon. I must admit, from having had several turkeys prepared this way, I can assure you, this is a recipe and cooking method worth trying!

1 12-15 Lb. Turkey
5 Gal. Vegetable Oil
Marinade:
4 Tbsp. seasoned salt, use recipe Chapter IV
2 Tbsp. White Pepper
1 Tbsp. Garlic Powder
1 Tbsp. Chili Powder
1 Tbsp. Cayenne Pepper
2 Bottles Non-Light Beer
¼ Cup Hot Sauce
½ Gal White Wine
½ Gal Water
1 Quart Olive Oil
6 Tbsp. Rosemary
6 Tbsp. Basil
2 Tbsp. Oregano
3 Tbsp. Fresh Cracked Black Pepper
2 Tbsp. Kosher Salt
1 Cup Garlic, Minced

Blend marinade items together evenly and place in large plastic bag. Place turkey in bag and marinade in refrigerator for 24 hours; place in a large pot to avoid spillage. Turn occasionally in bag to disperse marinade. Remove turkey and pat dry. Fry in oil at 350° for 45 minutes.

WILD PRAIRIE HEN WITH CRANBERRY GLAZE

A friend of mine requested that I include a recipe for Prairie Hen in this cookbook. He said that he was not sure if he liked Sage or Prairie Hen, as they never seemed to taste quite right, and seemed a little tough. My suggestion is to allow these birds to age, and soak them in a hearty three-wine marinade, adding a small amount of Pineapple juice, or Papaya juice to add to the softening and breakdown of the tissue.

Ingredients:
1 Medium/Large Prairie Hen
2 Cups of Celery, Chopped
1 Cup Onion, Chopped
2 Tablespoons Unsalted Butter
1 Tablespoon Cracked Black Pepper
1 Tablespoon Kosher Salt
1 Teaspoon Fresh Chopped Thyme
1 Teaspoon Fresh Chopped Parsley
1 Cups Cranberry Juice
1 Cups Red Wine
1/2 Cup Orange Juice
2 Cups Whole Cranberry's
1 Tablespoon of Fresh Lemon Juice
¼ Cup Sugar

Preparation: Rinse and pat dry Prairie Hen. Place into the body cavity chopped celery and onion, and truss closed with small piece of cotton string. Blend butter, pepper, salt, parsley, and thyme together, and rub the skin of the hen, evenly. Place hen into a baking dish, with wrack, covered loosely with aluminum foil, (to prevent scorching). Place hen into an oven and bake at 375 degrees for 45 minutes. In a saucepan, combine the cranberry juice, red wine, orange juice, and simmer for 20 minutes. Add the whole cranberries, lemon juice and sugar and continue to reduce until cranberries have softened and cooked. Remove from heat and keep warm. Check internal temperature of hen. When internal temperature has reached 165 degrees, remove foil, and allow to brown for 10 minutes. Remove hen from oven. Place on serving platter and garnish with fresh cranberries and orange zest. Serve the hen with cranberry glaze. For an appropriate dressing, try Sourdough, Apple-Sage Dressing with Almonds, located in Chapter XIV.

WOOD SMOKED DUCK BREAST BACON WRAPPED, IN BLUSH WINE SAUCE

If you are fortunate to have a good a good supply of duck, or have an outlet for good duck breast meat, then this is the recipe to try. If you do not have a smoker, there are a large number of "Liquid Smokes" and marinade combinations that will produce a fine wood smoked flavor. If the is a favorite flavor that I personally have, it is to slow smoke my game birds and waterfowl in a rich, natural wood smoke. It is a flavor this is out of this world!

Ingredients: 6 Large Duck Breasts, cleaned and rinsed.
2 Tbsp. Liquid Smoke
2 Cups Water
2 Cups of Rose or Blush Wine
1 Cup Fresh Game Bird Stock

1 Tbsp. Fresh Cracked Black Pepper
6 Slices of Smoked Bacon
1 Tsp. Kosher Salt
4 Tbsp. Unsalted Butter
2 Tbsp. Corn Starch to Thicken Sauce

Preparation: In a bowl add the water, liquid smoke and 1 cup of wine, blend and add the duck breasts to marinate for 24 hours, covered, in the refrigerator. Remove and pat dry the duck breasts. In a sauté pan, slowly melt the butter until it begins to brown. Add the duck breasts and slowly sauté, turning after 1 minute to sear in the moisture. When the duck breasts are lightly browned, (3 to 5 minutes) remove from the sauté pan, and when sufficiently cooled, wrap each breast with bacon, and pin with a tooth pick. Place in a small baking buttered baking dish, season with salt and pepper, and place into a 325 degree oven to finish cooking, and (20 to 30minutes). Using the same sauté pan that you seared the duck breast in, slowly reheat, adding one cup of wine, fresh game bird stock and reduce slowly by 1/3. When the sauce mixture has reduced, add the cornstarch mixture, and whisk until sufficiently thickened. Remove duck breasts from oven slice and serve with the blush sauce and garnish with orange zest.

STUFFED OVEN ROASTED CANADIAN HOLIDAY WILD GOOSE

During the holiday seasons, I have always had a turkey for Thanksgiving, and a traditional Christmas Goose. I have always felt that the holiday seasons are a special time in our family and that the meals and menus should reflect those times of good cheer. I have included this holiday favorite recipe in this cookbook with a request. Cook this dish with good cheer, and enjoy the meal with family, friends and loved ones. A warm hearth and home with family and friends is the greatest final to a great meal!

Ingredients: 12-15 lb. Canadian Goose, clean & dress
Marinade:
1 Gallon Water
½ Gallon Apple Cider
1 Quart Pear Nectar
2 Tbsp. Celery Salt
2 Tbsp. Garlic Powder
Stuffing:
4 Apples Cored, peeled & chopped
2 Pears Cores, Chopped
1 Large Onion, finely chopped
2 Cups Celery, finely chopped
1 Cup Raisins
1 Cup Walnut, finely chopped
10 Cups Dry Bread Crumbs
1-2 Cups Game Bird Stock
1/2 Tsp. Kosher Salt
1 Tbsp. Cracked Black Pepper
1 Tbsp. Garlic, Minced
1 Tbsp. Poultry Seasoning
1 Tsp. Sage
1 Tbsp. Rosemary
Goose Seasoning Rub:
2 Tsp. Kosher Salt
2 Tbsp. Wild Game Season-All
1 Tbsp. Cracked Black Pepper
1 Tsp. Paprika
½ Tsp. Garlic Powder
Basting Mixture:
2 Cups Apple Cider
1 Cup Pear Nectar
1 Cup Orange Juice
½ Cup Plum Nectar

Preparation: Place wash and cleaned goose into large bag or container, saturate with marinade and place cover in refrigerator for 24 hours. To prepare stuffing: mix thoroughly fruits, nuts, onion, celery, herbs, seasoning and stock as needed to moisten in a large bowl. Remove goose from marinade and fill body cavity with stuffing mixture. Close body cavity with cotton string. Combine seasoning rub ingredients in small bowl and run entire outer skin of goose coating evenly. Any remaining mixture hand sprinkle over breast area. Place goose on rack in a cover roaster at 400 degrees for 20 minutes. Prepare basting mixture and initially baste goose after first 20 minutes. Reduce heat to 325 degrees and slow roast allowing 20 minutes per pound. Baste with basting mixture every 15 minutes during roasting. Be advised to check internal temperature of both the goose and the stuffing to insure that both are thoroughly cooked. If the stuffing is not properly cooked you run the risk of a food borne illness. Preferred internal temperature of stuffing should exceed 165 degrees. If necessary remove stuffing and finish baking separately. Recommended serving with wild goose giblet gravy.

COMPLETING THE MEAL WITH SIDES!

Side dishes will make or break a meal. You can prepare and execute the finest main dish, and cripple the entire dining experience if you do not have a balance of flavors, colors or complimentary foods to accompany that main dish. All of your work will be for naught. Planning is the key to a fine meal. Plan your menu well, and the meal will be more of a dining treat. I have always felt that a good blend of flavors should accompany any dish to allow the home gourmet the greatest opportunity to make every meal an experience to remember. I have presented to you a selection of basic recipes, techniques, and flavors in this first book, to allow you to learn and employ some of the basics of gourmet game home cooking. You now have a varied menu of game recipes to choose from that should satisfy most tastes and choices. It is time to put these wonderful items together with a few favorites of mine to make a great dining experience, greater!

I have based the following selections on "old home recipes and ingredients", and have added a few twists and turns to allow them to become hotter and wilder. Some of the following recipes may be familiar in their basic contents and ingredients. I have always attempted to expand on the familiar, and keep my "gourmet tastes" within reason. I am sure you have seen or heard of new taste sensations, that would make the cat want to cover them up!

Most of us are truly, "meat and tatters" folks. In this introductory book, I have attempted to give you new and vibrant tastes, with standard, favorite ingredients. You will be amazed what you can accomplish with "beans, rice and tatters"!

I hope that you enjoy these selections. In my future cookbooks, which are due for publication soon, you will find one book dedicated to some of the most glorious side dishes, sauces and vegetables, to accompany game as you might desire! Pull up a pot, and "let's get to cookin"!

SWEET POTATOES WITH CRANBERRY GLAZE

Sweet potatoes are, considered by some, as a holiday dish. I believe that they should be enjoyed year round. I hope you enjoy this side starch with a zing!

Ingredients:
- 6 Medium Sweet Potatoes, Peeled, cut into 1-inch cubes
- ½ Cup Brown Cane Sugar
- 2 Tablespoons Butter
- 2 Tablespoons Orange Juice Concentrate
- 1 Cup Whole-Berry Cranberry Sauce
- ½ Teaspoon of Kosher Salt
- 2 Tablespoons of Orange Zest for Garnish
- 2 Tablespoons of Orange Liquor (Optional)

Preparation: Peel and cube the sweet potatoes. Place the sweet potatoes into a medium saucepan, add water to cover, add the kosher salt, and heat to a slow boil. You will cook the sweet potatoes until tender, (about 15-20 minutes at a slow boil). While the sweet potatoes cook, combine the brown sugar, butter, orange juice concentrate, and cranberry sauce into a small saucepan, cooking on low heat, stirring gently to blend all ingredients. If you wish to add the two optional tablespoons of Orange Liquor for an added flavor to the sauce, do so at this time. Simmer the sauce on low heat for 20 minutes. Remove and drain the sweet potatoes. Melt 1 tablespoon of butter and use it to grease a 9 x 11-inch baking dish. Add the sweet potatoes to the baking dish, adding the sauce, and tossing gently. Bake in the oven at 350 degrees for 30 minutes. When served, add the Orange Zest as a garnish

SWEET POTATOES WITH APPLES AND A MAPLE-PECAN GLAZE

This is a wonderful presentation dish for sweet potatoes. It not only tastes good; it also looks great on the plate. It has a subtle blend of flavors, which ads dimension to whatever type of game you serve. It is a complement to any meal!

Ingredients:
8 Tablespoons Butter
6 Medium Sweet Potatoes, (peeled & sliced ¼ inch thick)
6 Medium Apples (Granny Smith's are very good) halved, cored and
Sliced, ¼ inch thick
2 Cups of Pure Maple Syrup
1 & ½ Cups Apple Cider
4 Ounces Unsalted Butter
½ Cup Finely Chopped Pecans
1 Tablespoon of Honey

Preparation: Peel and slice the sweet potatoes. Peel, core, half and slice the apples. Melt two ounces of butter and grease a 9 x 11-inch baking dish. Alternate (shingle) the sweet potatoes and apples in the baking dish in a single layer. Sprinkle the kosher salt lightly over the apples and sweet potatoes. Combine the apple cider, maple syrup, 6 ounces of butter, and honey in a small saucepan and simmer for 5 to 10 minutes, stirring occasionally to blend all ingredients. Pour the sauce, evenly over the contents of baking dish, cover with aluminum foil. Place baking dish into a 350-degree oven and bake for 45 minutes. Add 4 ounces of unsalted butter to a small skillet and melt slowly. Add the chopped pecans and slowly sauté for 10 minutes. When the sweet potatoes and apples are ready, remove the baking dish from the oven. Glaze with the butter and sautéed pecans, turn the oven to 400 degrees, and continue to bake for 30 minutes, uncovered. Check the cooking progress until the sweet potatoes & apples are tender, and done.

ROASTED RED GARLIC POTATOES WITH SAUTED MUSHROOMS & ROSEMARY

I have always loved the taste of oven roasted potatoes. Red potatoes have always been a favorite of mine to work with as a chef. They make such a nice plate presentation, especially when tossed with a small amount of freshly sautéed mushrooms. I always add a few shakes of dried red pepper to this dish. I like my food to bite back! This ingredient is optional.

Ingredients:
- 2 Pounds of Fresh Red Potatoes
- 8 Oz of Fresh Sliced Mushrooms
- ¼ Cup of Virgin Olive Oil
- 3 Tablespoons Butter
- 2 Tablespoon Minced Garlic
- ¼ Cup finely Chopped Green Onion
- 1 Tablespoon Fresh Cracked Black Pepper
- 1 to 2 Tablespoons Garlic Powder
- ½ Tablespoon Onion Powder

1 Tablespoon Kosher Salt
(Dried Red Pepper, Optional, to Taste)
Fresh Whole Rosemary as Garnish

Preparation: Select and rinse two pounds of fresh Red Potatoes. Cut into halves or quarters depending on size of potatoes. Leave the skins on the potatoes. Place in a mixing bowl, and toss with ¼ cup olive oil. Place potatoes on a baking sheet pan, using any excess olive oil to grease the pan. Spread the potatoes evenly, and season with Kosher salt, Black Pepper, Garlic Powder, Onion Powder (and Red Pepper if desired). Place baking sheet into an oven and bake at 375 degrees for 45 minutes, or until tender. Place butter into a sauté pan and heat. When hot add chopped garlic and chopped green onion, quickly sautéing for 2 to 4 minutes. Add the sliced mushrooms, and sauté until tender (about 3 to 5 minutes). Remove potatoes from oven, serve, and top with sautéed mushrooms, garlic & onions. Garnish as desired with Rosemary.

PAN SAUTED CHILI POTATOES WITH MIXED PEPPERS

I love potatoes! I always have since I can remember, sitting next to my mom at the dinner table. That was one of the staples of our home when I was a kid, and my mother did not have to force me to eat. To this day, I enjoy working with "uncle spud" and have on file hundreds of potato recipes accumulated throughout my years as a chef. This is one of my favorites that I am about to share with you.

Ingredients: 2 Pounds (Large) Idaho Potatoes
½ Cup Olive Oil
2 Tablespoons Chile Powder

1Green Bell Pepper
1 Red Bell Pepper
1 Yellow Bell Pepper
2 Serrano Peppers, Finely Diced
2 Tablespoons Fresh Cracked Pepper
1 Tablespoon Kosher Salt
3 Tablespoons of Fresh Chives (as a garnish)

Preparation: Wash and thin slice the potatoes (1/4-inch thick slices) leaving the skins on. Evenly distribute potatoes on a baking sheet. Brush the potatoes with a light coating of olive oil, season with kosher salt, Fresh Cracked Black Pepper, and Chili Powder. Place in the oven and slow bake at 325 degrees for 15 to 20 minutes. Your goal is to "half bake" the potatoes, so that will finish cooking and browning with the peppers. Half the peppers and slice thin (1/4 inch thick), toss with olive oil, and slow sauté (over medium heat) in a large skillet or wok, (a wok works best for this dish). When the peppers are beginning to tenderize, remove the potatoes from the oven, and add to the sauté mixture. Toss every two minutes until both potatoes and peppers are tender. Check the potatoes for desired tenderness. Remove and plate. Add Fresh Chives as a garnish and serve.

WILD GAME STOCK RICE PILALF

I knew the chapter on game stocks would come in handy! This recipe is a basic rice dish that "gets carted out a whole new door" by the addition of fresh game stock. The blending of flavors, seasonings and the use of wild or brown rice not only makes this a beautiful presentation dish it is also very simple to prepare. I am sure that this will become a household favorite!

Ingredients: 2 Cups Long Grain, Wild Rice Blend

4 Cups of Wild Game Stock of Choice
2 Tablespoons of Unsalted Butter
¾ Cup of Minced Leeks
¼ Cup Chopped Green Onion Tops
1 Tablespoon of Minced Garlic
½ Cup of Sliced Fresh Mushrooms
1 Bay Leaf
1 Teaspoon of Fresh Cracked Black Pepper
Salt to taste. (Remember, your stock may have enough salt taste)

Preparation: Combine butter, leeks, green onion tops, garlic and pepper in a large skillet and lightly sauté on medium heat until the vegetables are translucent and moderately soft. Add the rice and continue to sauté, stirring frequently, ensuring that the rice is coated with butter, and are fully heated. Add the mushrooms, bay leaf and the stock to the skillet and simmer for two to three minutes, stirring the rice to prevent sticking. Transfer the pilaf to an oven safe, covered baking dish. Place into a pre-heated (375 degrees) and bake for 20 to 30 minutes. Check the rice after 20 minutes for tenderness, and remaining liquid, to ensure proper cooking. Rice should be tender, but not mushy. Rice should separate and "fluff" easily with a fork. There should be no liquids remaining at the bottom of the dish. When at desired texture, remove rice from the oven, fluff with a fork, and serve.

DOWN HOME VENISON RED BEANS AND RICE

This is a down home dish that is a real "Rib Sticker" You can season this dish to any desired level. This dish presents well, lends color to any plate, and goes with any meat, fish or fowl. This dish is a meal by itself. Not only is it pretty, but great tasting, too! I love versatility in cooking! This recipe will make 12 to 14 servings, or will feed at least six hungry hunters!

Ingredients:
4 Cups of Long Grain White Rice
8 Cups of White Game Stock
1 Pound of Red Beans, (Soaked in Water, Overnight)
1 Tablespoon Butter
½ Pound Salt Pork
3 Cups of Chopped Onion
1 & ½ Cups Chopped Green Onion
1 Cup of Fresh Chopped Parsley
1 Cup Medium Chopped Green Bell Pepper
2 Tablespoons Minced Garlic
1 Teaspoon of Kosher Salt
1 Teaspoon Red Pepper
1 Teaspoon Fresh Cracked Black Pepper
1 Tablespoon of Hot Sauce or Tabasco
1 Tablespoon of Worcestershire Sauce
¼ Cup Tomato Paste
¼ Teaspoon of Oregano
1 Teaspoon of Thyme
1 Pound of Ground Venison or Elk Sausage (for extra body and flavor)

Preparation: Soak red beans overnight in 2 quarts of water. Place rice in an oven safe pan. Add stock and 1 tablespoon of butter to a saucepan, and bring to a boil. Add stock to rice and oven back for 30 to 40 minutes at 375 degrees. Remove rice when finished cooking and place aside. When ready to cook red beans, drain the beans, add to a large pot, and add two quarts of fresh cold water. Add the salt pork whole, and cook beans over medium heat for 1 hour, stirring occasionally to prevent sticking. Add all other ingredients, except sausage, and cook on low heat for one more hour, stirring occasionally to prevent sticking. Add the sausage and cook on low heat for one more hour. Remove from heat, and serve over rice.

LOUISIANA PECAN "DIRTY RICE"

A chef friend from New Orleans gave me this recipe a long time ago. He had reduced rice dishes to an art form, and "dirty rice" was one of his specialties! I do not know what ever happened to Chef Joe, but I still have many of his recipes, that he had written down on napkins, and bits of paper. I hope you enjoy this dish. I have on many occasions.

Ingredients:
- 3 Cups of Brown Rice
- 6 Cups of Wild Game Stock (Game Bird or Duck Stock is preferred)
- 2 Cups of Finely Diced Green Bell Pepper
- 2 Cups of Finely Diced Onion
- 4 Stalks of Celery (tops included) finely diced
- ½ Pound of Chicken Livers
- ½ Cup diced Bacon or Ground Pork
- 1 Tablespoon of Minced Garlic
- 2 Tablespoons of Butter
- 2 Tablespoons of Bacon Drippings
- ¼ Cup of Finely Chopped Pecans
- 2 Tablespoons of Hot Sauce or Tabasco
- 1 Tablespoon of Worcestershire Sauce
- 1 Tablespoon of Cayenne Pepper
- 1 Teaspoon of Kosher Salt
- 1 Tablespoon of Fresh Cracked Pepper

Preparation: In a large oven safe pan, add rice. In a saucepan, add stock, one tablespoon of butter, and bring to a boil. Add stock to the rice, stir well, and place rice and stock in a 375-degree oven and bake covered for 20 to 30 minutes. Check rice after 20 minutes. Do not over cook the rice. In a large skillet, add the bell pepper, onion, celery, remaining butter, and bacon drippings. Sauté the vegetables over medium heat for 20 to 30 minutes, stirring occasionally. Add the chicken livers, pork or bacon, and cook until meat is done, then mash with a spoon or potato masher. The mixture should look "dirty" or muddy. If mixture is dry, add a small amount of melted butter and water. Add the remaining seasonings and pecans simmering for five minutes. Remove from heat, mix well with the rice, and serve.

SOURDOUGH APPLE-SAGE DRESSING WITH ALMONDS

Dressings and stuffing's are not only a great accompaniment with any game or fowl dish that you prepare, they allow you to use those left over rolls and breads that seem to multiply around the kitchen. I never purchase breadcrumbs or instant dressings. It is silly to spend the money. The best source of dressings, and breadcrumbs are thrown into the trash, daily. In large kitchens, hotels and restaurants chefs save their breads and roles, dry them, and grind them into breading. It has never seemed sensible to waste such a great source of raw product. For this recipe, I had leftover sourdough bread. The rest was imagination!

Ingredients:

1 &1/2 Pounds Sourdough Bread, (trim the Crusts cut into ½ inch cubes)
2 Cups Onions, Finely Chopped
1 Cup Celery, Finely Chopped
3 Medium Apples, Cored, peeled, and Finely Chopped
1 & ½ Cup Almonds, Finely Chopped
1 Tablespoon Fresh Parsley, Chopped

3 Tablespoons Fresh Sage, Finely Chopped
1 Tablespoon Freshly Cracked Black Pepper
1 Teaspoon Kosher Salt
4 Tablespoons, Fresh Rosemary
1/3 Cup Unsalted Butter
10 Slices of Bacon, Chopped
3 Large Eggs, Beaten
1 & ½ Cups Fresh White Game Stock
1/3 Cup Fresh Apple Cider

Preparation: After trimming the bread and cubing, place into an oven and toast until crisp and dry, (about 20 minutes). Remove the bread and place aside. In a small skillet, add the finely chopped almonds, one teaspoon of butter and slowly sauté until toasted and golden in color. Place aside. In a large skillet, add the bacon and sauté for 10 minutes, or until golden brown. Add to the same skillet, the remaining butter, the celery, onions, and apples and slowly sauté until "clear" or translucent. In a mixing bowl, add the bread, sautéed bacon and vegetables, almonds, herbs and seasonings, (do not add the Rosemary). Add 3 beaten eggs, apple cider, and enough game stock to moisten, and mix by hand. Ensure that all ingredients are evenly blended. In a greased pan, add the dressing, evenly and bake at 375 degrees for 20 minutes, covered. Uncover dressing, and bake for 20 additional minutes, or top is crisp and lightly browned. Serve and garnish with fresh rosemary.

BABY CARROTS SAUTED WITH PEPPERS, MUSHROOMS, AND GARLIC

Many vegetable recipes are complex, and many are grand in their simplicity. This is one of those "simply grand" recipes. I have served this dish many times in my professional career, and it always, was well received, by my customers.

Ingredients: 1 Pound of Fresh Baby Carrots
¼ Cup Finely Diced Green Bell Pepper
¼ Cup Finely Diced Red Bell Peppers
¼ Cup Thinly Sliced Mushrooms
1 Tablespoon of Minced Garlic
3 Tablespoons of Butter
1 Teaspoon Fresh Dill
1 Teaspoon of Kosher Salt
1 Teaspoon of Fresh Cracked Black Pepper

Preparation: Rinse, and steam the baby carrots until they are tender, but firm. Drain, and place aside. Add all other ingredients, (except dill) and sauté over medium heat, (about five minutes) allowing the vegetables to soften and sweat. Add the baby carrots and toss to blend all ingredients well. You will sauté for about 3 minutes. Remove from heat, serve, and garnish with fresh dill.

JALAPENO & LIME MARINATED GRILLED VEGETABLES WITH PEPPER SAUCE

This recipe will light your fire! If you love fresh grilled seasonal vegetables, that has bite, then this is the recipe you want to try! I will warn you, this is a great recipe for that hot and wild person in your life. This vegetable dish is great with any game meat. It also may be expanded, to make a wild appetizer plate! When my cooks would prepare this dish, I would tell them, "Let's get hot and grill! Thrill some people! Cook it hot, boys and girls!"

Ingredients: 3 Large Portabella Mushrooms
1 Large Zucchini
1 Large Yellow Squash

1 Large Bell Pepper
1 Large Red Bell Pepper
1 Large Yellow Bell Pepper
1 Large Red Onion
1 Large Yellow Onion
¼ Cup Balsamic Vinegar
1/3 Cup Olive Oil
1/3 Cup Fresh Lemon Juice
2/3 Cup Fresh Lime Juice
4 Tablespoons of Course Chopped Garlic
2 Roma Tomatoes, de-seeded, finely diced
1 Teaspoon Chili Powder
3 Tablespoons Fresh Cracked Black Pepper
1 Teaspoons Kosher Salt
4 Tablespoons Chopped Cilantro
2 Jalapeno Peppers, finely diced, & de-seeded
1/3 Cup Honey
4 Tablespoons Spicy Brown Mustard

Preparation: Rinse and pat dry your selection of vegetables. Slice the vegetables lengthwise ¼ inch in thickness. When cutting the peppers, core and clean them. Make one full cut; then flatten the peppers out and cut into ½ wide strips. Cut the onion into quarters, and lance with a small skewer to hold them together while grilling. To prepare the marinade, combine the following ingredients in a bowl. 1 finely diced Jalapeno pepper, 2 tablespoons of minced garlic, 2 tablespoons of fresh Cilantro, 1 teaspoon of chili powder, 5 tablespoons of olive oil, 8 tablespoons of lime juice, 2 tablespoons of lemon juice, 1 tablespoon of fresh cracked black pepper, 1 teaspoon of kosher salt, 2 tablespoons of balsamic vinegar, and whisk briskly for one minute. Place vegetables in a large mixing bowl and ad the marinade. Toss the vegetables, coating the vegetables, and let stand for 30 minutes to 1 hour before grilling. In a saucepan, combine the remaining ingredients, except the tomatoes, and heat very slowly on low heat. This sauce is not to be cooked, just warmed. Whisk the sauce to blend all ingredients evenly. Grill the vegetables, directly from the marinade over low coals, or on a low grill setting. Do not over cook the vegetables. They should be tender, with good grill marks. Before serving, ladle the sauce over the vegetables and garnish with the tomatoes.

GRILLED EGGPLANT WITH GINGER BUTTER

Eggplant, when lightly grilled is a treat. I have met many people who think that eggplant is only prepared by covering it with breadcrumbs, frying it, and burying it with sauce. This recipe is wonderful when the eggplant is grilled, or pan-sautéed. I enjoy this dish grilled with a touch of ginger butter added for that special flavor.

Ingredients:
- 1 Large, Fresh Eggplant
- ¼ Cup Olive Oil
- 1 Tablespoon Fresh Cracked Black Pepper
- 1 Teaspoon of Kosher Salt
- 2 Tablespoons Fresh Gingerroot, finely grated
- 1 stick (1/4 pound) Butter

Preparation: Place butter into a bowl or mixer and whip until soft. Combine kosher salt, black pepper and gingerroot, and whip together until blended well. Remove butter from bowl, and place on a piece of plastic wrap. Form into the shape of a log, by forming and hand rolling. Place butter into the refrigerator and chill to set. Peal and cut the eggplant into ¼ thick slices. Brush with olive oil and grill over low heated coals until tender. If you are pans sautéing, brush both the pan and eggplant with a light coat of olive oil, and cook over medium heat until tender and brown. Remove butter and cut into small medallions. Serve eggplant hot with a pat of ginger butter. Salt and pepper to taste.

OVEN BROILED TOMATOES WITH GARLIC, FETA & OLIVES

If you like tomatoes with a twist of seasonings and cheese, this you will enjoy. A simple side dish to prepare, broiled tomatoes are limited only by your imagination. This is one of many of my tomato recipes. Enjoy!

Ingredients:
- 2 Large, Vine Ripened Tomatoes
- 4 Tablespoons Olive Oil
- 1 Cup Feta Cheese
- 2 Tablespoons Minced Garlic
- 4 Tablespoons Minced Black Olives
- 2 Tablespoons Minced Kalamata Olives
- ¼ Teaspoon Kosher Salt
- 1 Tablespoon Fresh Cracked Black Pepper
- Fresh Rosemary to Garnish

Preparation: Rinse and cap tomatoes, then pat dry. Half the tomatoes at center point, equally. Brush olive oil on the entire tomato halves. Gently sprinkle with salt and pepper. Place into the oven and broil until tomatoes are "fork tender", but not soft. Remove from the oven and top with Feta cheese and olives. Return to the oven and allow cheese to melt evenly on the tomatoes. Remove from the oven, and garnish with a few leaves of fresh Rosemary, and serve.

SEASONED FRIED ZUCCHINI WITH PEPPER AND TOMATO VINAIGRETTE

A simple variation, on a traditional zucchini recipe, by adding a fresh and spicy vinaigrette. I serve this tomato/pepper vinaigrette warm for dinner, and serve the remainder chilled, with a fresh, field greens salad.

Ingredients:
3 Medium, Fresh Zucchini
1 Cup Flour
1 Cup Beer
½ Teaspoon Kosher Salt
1 Tablespoon Cracked Black Pepper
½ Teaspoon Garlic Powder
½ Teaspoon Onion Powder
½ Teaspoon Cayenne Pepper
1 Tablespoon Basil
4 Cups Olive Oil (for frying)

Ingredients for Vinaigrette:
1 Cup Olive Oil
¼ Cup Balsamic Vinegar
¼ Cup Red Bell Pepper
¼ Cup Green Bell Pepper
½ Teaspoon Hot Sauce
1 Teaspoon Fresh Thyme, finely minced
1 Teaspoon Fresh Basil, finely minced
2 Tablespoons Tomato Paste
2 Tablespoons warm water
1 Teaspoon Capers, (drained)
¼ Teaspoon Cracked Black Pepper
¼ Teaspoon Kosher Salt

Preparation: Prepare the vinaigrette first. Finely mince the red & green bell peppers, place into a mixing bowl, and add all other vinaigrette ingredients. Using a whisk, blend all ingredients for two minutes, and let stand in your refrigerator for 1 to 2 hours to "rest", allowing the flavors to combine. Rinse and cut the zucchini into medallions (1/4 inch thick). In a mixing bowl, add the beer, herbs and seasonings, and last, the flour. Mix with a heavy whisk until well blended, and the batter is smooth in consistency. In a skillet, add 4 cups of olive oil, and heat on medium. Before frying, always test the oil by cooking a small portion of batter for proper oil temperature. In small batches, batter the zucchini, and place into the oil, cooking to a rich golden brown color. Remember to turn the zucchini to cook evenly. When finished frying the zucchini, place on a rack and towel to absorb the excess oil. Place the rack on a sheet pan, and place into the oven at 275 degrees to finish browning. Place the vinaigrette in a small saucepan and slowly heat. Do not cook the vinaigrette. Remove zucchini and serve with vinaigrette.

BROCCOLI WITH ROASTED PEPPERS AND OLIVES

This is a very simple dish to prepare. This is a fast gourmet recipe that will go well with any game dish that you prepare. It also has the side benefit of being a healthy dish for those who are watching there waste lines!

Ingredients:
- 6 Cups of Fresh Broccoli Florets
- 1 Red Bell Pepper
- 1 Green Bell Pepper
- 1 Yellow Bell Pepper
- ¼ Teaspoon Fresh Cracked Black Pepper
- 1 Tablespoon of Minced Garlic
- 2 Tablespoons Lemon Zest
- 1 Tablespoon Lemon Juice
- ½ Cup Sliced Black Olives
- 2 Tablespoons Olive Oil

Preparation: Rinse and cut bell peppers in half. Remove the seeds and membranes. Place the bell peppers on a small baking sheet (skin sides up) and broil for 10 minutes, or until the peppers, are blackened. Remove the peppers from the oven and place them into a zip lock bag, and let them stand for 30 minutes to allow the skins to loosen, and peel. Cut the peppers into ¼ inch wide strips. Combine the garlic, black olives, pepper and olive oil in a medium skillet. On medium heat, slowly sauté the mixture until garlic is soft, (about five minutes). Add the peppers and heat for 3 to 5 minutes on low heat. Arrange broccoli florets and steam for 3 to five minutes, or until tender. Add with peppers, and toss to mix. Garnish with lemon zest, and serve.

LEMON SAUTED SPINICH AND GREENS WITH SESAME SEEDS

This is another simple gourmet dish that is served with any meat, fowl or fish dish. This is great for those who like to "fast sauté" and serve directly to the table. I have a friend that actually prepares this dish at tableside. It is a great show to impress the neighbors. Do not set fire to the curtains! It spoils the meal.

Ingredients:
- 3 Teaspoons Sesame Seeds
- 2 Tablespoons of Olive Oil
- ½ Pound of Greens (Beet Greens are good)
- ½ Pound of Fresh Spinach, stems removed
- ¼ Tablespoon Lemon Juice
- ¼ Tablespoon Lemon Zest
- ½ Teaspoon Kosher Salt
- 1 Teaspoon of Fresh Cracked Black Pepper

Preparation: Rinse and pat dry the greens and spinach. Remove the stems from the spinach. Trim the beet greens, and cut into small strips, (about 2-inch strips). Place the sesame seeds into a dry skillet. Heat over medium heat for 3 minutes or until fragrant. Remove seeds and place onto a cutting board. Coarsely crush the seeds with the flat side of a knife. Heat the olive oil in the same skillet. Add the greens in equal batches, (half spinach/half greens) and sauté over medium heat until "wilted" (about 3 minutes). Stir in lemon juice, lemon zest and sesame seeds. Season with salt and fresh milled black pepper. Serve hot with garnish.

ASPARAGUS WITH LEMON-BALSAMIC VINAIGRETTE

This is a favorite around my kitchen. I enjoy preparing this dish because everyone in our household loves it! This dish is a simple dish to prepare, and presents well on a large plate.

Ingredients:
- 2 Pounds of Fresh Asparagus
- ¼ Cup Olive Oil
- ¼ Cup Balsamic Vinegar
- 3 Tablespoons of Fresh Rosemary
- 2 Teaspoons Fresh Lemon Zest
- 1 Teaspoon Fresh Cracked Black Pepper
- ½ Teaspoon of Kosher Salt

Preparation: Add olive oil, lemon zest, balsamic vinegar and pepper into a small saucepan. Whisk and blend for a minute, and place aside. Rinse and trim the bottoms of the asparagus. Sprinkle asparagus with salt and steam until tender. Heat the vinaigrette until warm. Do not cook the vinaigrette. Serve the asparagus with warm vinaigrette, and garnish with fresh rosemary.

ROASTED VEGETABLES WITH APPPLE WINE SAUCE

My grand dad was a farmer. He planted by the signs, with the Farmers' Almanac in one hand, and black earth in the other. He was a man of the earth, and grew the most beautiful gardens. He kept the family feed, and as a small boy, I would be at his side helping as I could. This recipe was one of his garden favorites.

Ingredients:
- 4 Cups Fresh Apple Cider
- 4 Fresh, Large Baking Apples
- 1&1/4 Cups of White Wine (semisweet)
- 4 Tablespoons Unsalted Butter
- 1 Pound Turnips
- 1 Pound Parsnips
- 1 Pound Carrots
- 1 Pound Rutabagas
- 1 Large Onion
- 1 Pound Fresh Yams
- 1 Tablespoon Fresh Cracked Black Pepper
- 1 Teaspoon of Kosher Salt

Preparation: Add apple cider and wine to a saucepan, and reduce (boil) until you have 1 cup of reduced sauce (about 30 minutes). Add butter one tablespoon at a time, whisking briskly. Peel apples and vegetables, cutting into ½ inch pieces. Place vegetables into a roasting pan, adding the apple-wine sauces, and mix until contents is coated. Sprinkle with salt and pepper, and place into a 375-degree oven and slow roast. Check vegetables and apples with a fork (about 30 minutes) until tender and golden brown. Garnish with sprig of fresh Basil, Parsley or Rosemary for plate presentation.

PAN SAUTED GREEN BEANS WITH ROSEMARY, ALMONDS AND MUSHROOMS.

Green beans are one of the standard side dishes in American cuisine. I have seen many variations and combinations for this vegetable, and you can create, or couple many of your own recipes with a few ingredients, and limitless imagination. I have always kept my green bean creations at a simple level. I enhance the flavor of the beans, but try not to detract from the flavor, or presentation. For this dish, less is more!

Ingredients:
- 1 to 2 pounds Fresh Green Beans
- 1 Cup Small Mushrooms, Thinly Sliced
- 1/3 Cup Sliced Almonds
- 3 Tablespoons Fresh Rosemary
- 2 Tablespoons Unsalted Butter
- 1 Teaspoon Fresh Cracked Black Pepper
- 1 Tablespoon Red Wine

Preparation: Rinse and remove the stems from the green beans, (snapping the ends is best), and allow to dry. In a small skillet, add one tablespoon of butter and almonds. On low heat, slowly sauté, lightly browning the almonds. In a large separate skillet, add one tablespoon of butter, red wine and slowly melt on low heat. Add the green beans, slowly sautéing and tossing to ensure even cooking. Cook the green beans until tender, but still crisp. Add the rosemary and mushrooms, tossing to mix and allow to sauté, slowly (about 5 minutes). Do not over cook the green beans and mushrooms. Add the sautéed almonds, tossing again to mix. Sprinkle with cracked black pepper, and serve.

PAN SAUTED, BALSAMIC & HERB GARDEN BLEND VEGETABLES

This perky little dish is very good with fish and fowl. It is light enough as a side with a Pesto Grilled Salmon, or with a stuffed quail or pigeon dish. I like to add a little Risotto, a light garden salad, a soft red wine or Chianti, and complete the meal with a small tiramisu and coffee. If you would like to have a true "rural Italian feast", this is the meal to create!

Ingredients:

2 Small Zucchini
2 Small Yellow Summer Squash
4 Roma Tomatoes, De-seeded and Large diced
1 Medium Green Bell Pepper
1 Medium Red Bell Pepper
1 Small Red Onion
2 Portabella Mushrooms
1 Cup Medium Mushrooms, Thinly Sliced
1 Small Eggplant
½ Cup Black Olives (drained and sliced)
¼ Cup Water
¼ Cup Red Wine
1 Tablespoon Unsalted Butter
1 Tablespoon Minced Garlic
2 Tablespoons Tomato Paste
2 Tablespoons Fresh Chopped Parsley
¼ Cup Fresh Basil, Chopped
1 Tablespoon Fresh Thyme, Minced
1 Teaspoon Fresh Rosemary, Minced
1 Tablespoon Fresh Cracked Black Pepper
1 Teaspoon Kosher Salt
2 Tablespoons Balsamic Vinegar
¼ Cup Olive Oil

Preparation: Peel the eggplant, and cut into ¼ inch thick medallions. Cap and cut the zucchini and summer squash into ¼ thick medallions. Cap and de-seed the peppers, cutting into ¼ inch wide slices. Thin slice the mushrooms. Brush clean and cut the Portabella mushrooms into ¼ inch thick slices. Cut the red onion into ½ inch cubes. Chop the Roma Tomatoes into ¼ inch sized pieces. In a small skillet, on low heat, add butter, and garlic, slowly sautéing, (for about 5 minutes). In a small saucepan, add the water and red wine. Bring to a fast boil, reduce the heat to low and stir in the tomato paste and sautéed garlic. Brush the vegetables with olive oil, and place on to a small baking sheet. Place into the oven and slow roast (at 325 degrees) until vegetables are tender. Remove the finished vegetables from the oven, separate the eggplant and keep warm. Place the remaining vegetables into a large skillet, add herbs and seasonings, tomato sauce, heat on low and toss to blend. In a small skillet, add balsamic vinegar, remaining olive oil and Roma tomatoes, gently sautéing on low heat. Place the eggplant medallions on a plate, spoon the vegetables, sauce over the eggplant, and top with the warm oil/balsamic vinegar and tomato garnish. For a final garnish, add a tablespoon of freshly grated Parmesan Cheese, and a sprig of Basil.

DESSERTS TO DIE FOR

There are thousands of kinds of desserts and they are all good. Very, very good and everyone loves dessert. One of the most often asked questions at the dinner table is: "What's for dessert." Across the past two hundred years many people on a world wide basic has come to love chocolate so there is a recipe for a great chocolate cake. When the pilgrims first came to America, they ate wild game every day and for dessert, they most often had apple or berry pie with the meal.

When I was a boy, we made fruit pies very often. My elder brother had a pecan pie that was the most wonderful you could every want to taste. So, in this chapter I put in the recipe for his pie. You can not have a good pie without a good crust so I start with two recipes for a good flaky crust.

MAMA'S BASIC PIE CRUST

Warm Crust

No substitutions in this recipe. You can not use oil in place of shortening or lard. The reason for this is that when you mix the shortening it is not completely blended. There will be small flakes in the mixture and these flakes melt during the backing process giving the crust its flakiness.

The recipe if for one piecrust that can be cooked in a pan or in glass, as you may desire. This is for and 8 or 9" pan.

1-1/4 cups flour
1/4 cup of ice water
1/2 teaspoon salt

1/3 cup chilled shortening or lard

Put the flour, salt and shortening into a mixing bowl and mix until the ingredients look like a course meal. Sprinkle the water into the mix a little at a time. Just until the mix holds together. Put on a lightly floured rolling board and make a ball. Roll the ball until it is about 1" thick. Take a knife and cut into a circle about 3" larger than the pan you are using. To transfer this to the pan you put the rolling pin in the middle of the circle and fold one side across the top of the rolling pin. The put over the pie pan and flop it into place. Press the dough into place in the pan and if there are any holes fill them in with left over scraps. Cut off the excess crust around the edges of the pan leaving about 1" hanging over. Then you crimp to the edges of the pan with your fingers or a fork, as you may desire.

Now it is time to bake the piecrust; so heat the oven to 450oF. Put holes in the crust with a fork on the sides and bottom. Bake 10-14 minutes or until the edges are tan.

MAMA'S BASIC PIE CRUST
Cold Method

The previous piecrust was for those pies that do not have a pastry cover or use pastry as ropes or decoration on top of the pie. This piecrust has more in ingredients in it and makes more dough. As in the previous piecrust, this will make one crust for and 8-9" pie tin.

2 cups flour
6 tablespoons ice water
1 teaspoon salt

3/4 cup chilled shortening or lard

We will now do the same thing as the Warm Method. We will mix the flour, salt and shortening until it is like course meal. When we add the water a little at a time until the pastry holds together. Take one half the mixture and sit aside. The other half is rolled out just as above and put in pie tin. The half that was sitting aside is rolled into a ball; both are covered loosely and put in the refrigerator while you prepare the filling. After you have prepared the filling, filled the pie tin, take the unused dough, and roll it out to make the top. You may then cover the top (but if you do cut holes in the top to let the steam out as the pie cooks.) You could cut into strips and do plain lattice, you could do twisted lattice, woven lattice, do spirals or twist or a thousand things. It is up to you.

MAMA'S BASIC OIL PIE CRUST

This recipe is for those people who desire to cook with oil rather than lard or shortening. It is my suggestion that if you are cooking with oil you use extra virgin olive oil. This recipe will make two crusts for a 8" or 9" pie tin, or a double crust.

2 cups flour
1/2 cut olive oil
1 teaspoon of salt
1/4 cup ice water

Mix the flour and the salt together. Blend the ice water and oil together and whip with whisk until creamy. Pour the wet blend into the flour and stir until it is dough. If it is a little dry add a few drops of oil; if it is too wet add flour. Roll into a ball as in all the other recipes and cut in half. On a lightly floured board, with a rolling pin, start in the middle and roll outwards. Roll to a circle that is about 3" larger than the pie pan you are using. Put your dough in the pan and press down with our fingers. Put the filling in the pie shell then roll out the other half of the dough and use it as you desire. Remember to leave enough space for steam to escape during the cooking process. Bake according to the recipe.

COMMENTS:

Above are the three basic flaky pastry crust that I use in making pies. These are used all over the world for making pies. In Mama's warm crust method, the bottom of the crust may bubble up during the backing process. If this happen you can put wax paper over the crust before you start baking and fill the crust with dried beans or dried black-eyed peas. This will hold the crust in place and you will have a perfect crust. After the banking keep the beans or peas, they are still good but they will need a longer soak than normal before cooking. When baking pies put a piece of foil under the pie pan to catch the drippings.

MAMA'S APPLE PIE

This is the standard recipe for apple pie that we cooked when is was a young boy. It was easy and tasted great every time. There is no such thing as bad apple pie. It is just that some are better than others. This recipe makes 8 servings. For this pie, we use the crust recipe from Mama's cold method.

6 medium-size cooking apples
1 cup of sugar
2 tablespoons butter or margarine
2 teaspoons lemon juice

1/4 teaspoon salt
1/8 teaspoon nutmeg
1/4 teaspoon cinnamon

Preheat the oven to 450oF. Prepare the crust as indicated in the crust recipe. Put crust in pie pan and cover with damp cloth while you prepare the filling. Prepare the top crust, set aside and also cover with damp cloth. Peel and core, the apples and cut into thin strips. Taste them, as sugar to your taste, then add the salt, nutmeg, cinnamon and lemon juice. Put into the pastry shell and flake butter here and there. Cover with the other dough and crimp around the edges. Cut holes in top dough so steam will escape. If you desire a glaze on top crust, brush with milk and sprinkle with sugar. Cook 20 minutes at 450o and then reduce heat to 375o and cook an additional 25-30" or until crust is browned. Let it cook 5-10" and serve. You may desire to serve this with ice cream or a good sharp cheddar cheese. Be careful it may still be too hot to eat at 10 minutes. Before the ice cream or this cheese, this is about 400 calories per slice.

BASIC FRESH FRUIT PIES

My favorite fresh fruit pie is peach, with cherry in second place. This recipe can be used for grape, plum, pear or any fresh fruit. This is a standard pie that makes 8 servings. These pies are cooked in uncooked pie shells so use Mama's cold crust.

1 quart fresh fruit, slice, pit and peel
1 cup of sugar
1/4 cup flour
2 table spoons olive oil
2 tablespoons butter

1/4 teaspoon nutmeg, ginger, cinnamon, or almond extract

Preheat the oven to 450oF. Make the pie crust from the cold crust method. Put in 8" or 9" pie pan and do not trim the edges. Place the fruit in a bowl add in all the other ingredients and mix well. Then pour into your pie shell and put flakes of butter in various places. Roll out the second half of the shell and put over the top cutting holes to let the steam out. Fold the top and bottom shells together, trim and crimp the edges with a fork or your fingers if you desire. For a great looking top crust, brush with milk and sprinkle with sugar. Remember to put a piece of foil on the rack below the pie to ketch the drippings. Bake 45 minutes until it is bubbling and brown. Let cool 10 minutes before cutting. Be careful it may be too hot to eat. If serving hot you can use ice cream on top. These are about 425 calories with out the ice cream.

PUMPKIN PIE

This type of pie has been made in America since the Pilgrims arrived. It is my understanding the Pilgrims found this melon growing wild in the forest. I like pumpkin pies and have made hundreds of them across the years. This recipe makes 8 servings and is made in an uncooked pie shell, so use Mama's cold method pie shell.

1-1/2 cups canned pumpkin
1-1/2 cups of evaporated skim milk
1 teaspoon vanilla extract
1/2 teaspoon grated orange rind
3 egg whites, slightly beaten
1/2 teaspoon nutmeg
1/2 teaspoon cinnamon

1/2 teaspoon ground ginger
2/3 cup of sugar
A pinch of ground cloves
1/2 cup brandy

Into a bowl place the pumpkin, and mix in the milk, extract, rind, and egg whites, stir until well blended. Add to this mixture the nutmeg, cinnamon, ginger, sugar and cloves. Beat until smooth. Then pour the brandy in and fold it into the mixture. Pour into an unbaked pie shell and bake 10 minutes at 450oF, then reduce the heat to 325oF and bake for an additional 45 minutes. If you can insert a knife into the middle of the pie and it comes out clean the pie is ready. Remember, let it cool a few minutes. Do not get burned.

CARL'S PECAN PIE

My brother is named Carl as you can see. When I was small he was the pie cook at home and I always loved this one. It makes a serving for 8 persons. It is baked in the uncooked shell. So, use Mama's cold crust method.

3 Cups pecans, the highest quality you can find
1 cup black molasses
1/4 cup of honey
4 tablespoons butter
3 eggs, beaten
1 teaspoon vanilla
1/2 teaspoon of salt

Mix the molasses, honey, butter, eggs, vanilla and salt. Mix well. Hold out 1 cup of the pecans and mix 2 cup in the mixture. Turn the mixture into an unbaked piecrust. Arrange 1 cup of whole pecans on top of the mixture, starting at the outer edge and working into the center in ever smaller circles. Bake at 425oF for 10 minutes then reduce heat to 325 and bake for 20 minutes more, or until a knife will come out clean. Let cool before eating. Very good if served warm with ice cream.

FRESH RHUBARB PIE

This recipe makes 8 servings, and the crust is Mama's cold crust method.

> 2 pounds rhubarb, trimmed and cut into 1/2" chunks
> 1-1/2 cups honey
> 2 tablespoons butter
> 1/3 flour
> 1/8 teaspoon salt

Roll out the pie shells and put one in an 8" - 9" baking tin, with the other you roll it out into a 12" circle and cut steam holes. Toss the rhubarb with the honey, butter, flour and salt. Pour into the pie shell. Flake with butter. Put the top cover on and fold over rhubarb, crimp the edges and brush the top with milk and sprinkle with sugar if you desire a shinny piecrust. Now remember to put the foil under the pie to ketch the drippings. Cook about 45 minutes at 425oF or until golden brown. About 490 calories per serving.

BRANDIED MINCEMEAT PIE

This is the easiest pie to make of all the pies. This pie makes 8 servings. The crust is uncooked and uses Mama's cold method.

> 1 - 12once jar mincemeat
> 6 tablespoons brandy

Empty the mincemeat into a strainer set over a bowl, let drain. Retain the liquid in the bowl you will use it later. Let drain 10-12 minutes. Mix enough brandy to suit your taste and spoon this mixture into the shell you have prepared. Pour some of the saved liquid, to just cover the mincemeat. Fit top crust over the pie, trim and crimp the edges. Start cooking at 450oF for 10 minutes and then reduce the heat to 350oF for 25 minutes or until lightly browned. Serve with an extra sharp cheddar.

KEY LIME PIE

This Florida Keys classic, has hundreds of variations but is a cream pie in a precooked pie shell. Use Mama's warm crust method. This makes 8 servings.

1 cup fresh lime juice
4 egg yokes, beaten
10 oz. sweetened condensed milk

Make the pie crust as indicated and bake and sit aside to cool as you mix the filling. Mix the eggs and the milk and stir until smooth, stir in the lime juice. Pour into the pie shell, Chill well then cover with whipped cream. Chill several more hours before serving. About 500 calories per serving.

CAKES

First may I say there are some great cake mixes in supermarkets these days that are easy to prepare. If you are short of time, you may desire to consider one of these mixes.

There are three kinds of cakes, soft and sponge cakes are the angel food, the chiffon cakes, and the true sponge. The second more firm cakes and muffins, the third is the conventional which is a very firm cake. Most cakes you see are the firm conventional cakes.

The conventional cakes are sometimes referred to as butter cakes. These contain butter, cream, soda or baking powder to leaven the cake. The second less firm cake is often called the one bowl cake for that reason. The sponge cakes are made with egg whites or many eggs, and are said to be air-leavened cakes. The chiffon cakes are a combination of the other two types; these have some eggs and some butter or cooking oil.

Since I like my chocolate cake best I will put that recipe first.

BEST CHOCOLATE CAKE

The way I make this is to add a little alcohol for flavor but it is not necessary for the great flavor of this cake. This is optional. This makes 8 servings.

- 2 cups of flour
- 2 cups of honey
- 1 teaspoon baking soda
- 3 tablespoons cocoa
- 1/4 cup buttermilk
- 2 eggs
- 1 teaspoon vanilla
- 1 cup hot water
- 1/2 cup shortening
- 1/4 lb. butter

Mix the flour, soda, and cocoa together. In another mixing bowl mix the honey, buttermilk, eggs, vanilla, water, shortening and butter. Pour the wet ingredients into the dry ones; mix thoroughly and pour into a buttered baking tin. Preheat the oven to 425oF and bake 20 minutes.

ICING:

1 box powdered sugar
1/2 coconut, ground
1/2 cup raisins
1/2 cup nuts (walnuts, pecans, etc)
1/4 lb. butter
3 tablespoons cocoa
6 tablespoons canned milk

In a saucepan mix the butter, milk and cocoa, bring to a boil, set aside and mix in the rest of the ingredients. Beat until stiff. You may desire to do the optional step before spreading the icing over the cake. If you do not use the option, then ice the cake and let set a few minutes before cutting.

(OPTIONAL) With the handle of a whisk punch 6 or 8 holes in the top of the cake, but not near the edges.

1 cup of chocolate syrup
6 tablespoons "Tia Maria"

Mix the syrup and the "Tia Maria" together until blended. Pour the mixture into the holes. Then put the icing on the cake. If you like some other liquor better than "Tia Maria" for this purpose then use that liquor. Many liquors are stronger in taste than other so you will have to determine what is best for you. If using "Jack Daniel's" use only 4 tablespoons.

CHOCOLATE BUNDT CAKE

A bundt cake is a round cake served upside down with a hole in the middle and usually with a sauce over the cake. This recipe makes 8 servings.

THE CAKE:

1 package fudge cake mix
1 - 3oz pkg., instant fudge Jell-O pudding mix
1 - 12 oz pkg. chocolate chips
1/2 cup olive oil
1/2 cup Kalhua or 1/2 warm water
1/2 cup sour cream
3 eggs or 3 egg whites

Mix all the ingredients together and pour into a well buttered and floured bundt pan. Preheat the oven to 375oF and bake for 50 minutes. Serve warm with the sauce.

THE SAUCE:

1 cup heavy whipping cream, stiff
3/4 cup honey
3 eggs yokes
1/2 teaspoon vanilla
1/4 teaspoon salt

Combine the honey, yolks, vanilla and salt, mix well, and fold in the whipping cream. Chill while making the cake.

APPLESAUCE CAKE

Apples are very good for you and this easy to make cake is also very good. This recipe makes 8 servings.

2 cups of flour
1 cup honey
1-3/4 cups applesauce (or 1-1lb can)
1 cup chopped nuts or raisins
1/2 cup butter
1 teaspoon salt
1 teaspoon baking soda
1 teaspoon cinnamon
1/2 teaspoon nutmeg
1/4 teaspoon ground cloves

In a large saucepan, melt the butter, remove from heat and blend in all of the remaining ingredients until completely combined. Pour into a 9" to 11" pan, which has been greased on the bottom only. Bake at 375oF for 30 minutes. Can be served warm with ice cream of whipped cream. Can also be served cold.

OATMEAL CAKE

Recent studies have proven that oatmeal is very good for you. This oatmeal cake is very good also. The recipe makes 8 servings.

THE CAKE:

1 cup quick oatmeal
1 cup boiling water
1 cup honey
1 cup brown sugar
1/4 lb. butter
1-3/4 cups flour
2 eggs (beaten)
1 teaspoon baking soda
3 teaspoons cinnamon
1/4 teaspoon salt

Mix the oatmeal into the boiling water in a bowl and let stand for 10 minutes. Cream together the honey, sugar, butter, then add in the eggs. Mix the flour, soda, cinnamon, salt and add the oatmeal mixture and the honey etc. Preheat the oven to 375oF and bake for 45 minutes.

THE FROSTING:

1-1/2 cups coconut
3/4 cups honey
1 cup chopped nuts
1/4 cup cream
1 teaspoon vanilla

Mix all items together and spread on the cake, slide under the broiler to toast frosting.

SPICE CAKE

This is a wonderful cake with great taste. Many kinds of nuts and fruits can be used in the case along with liquor (optional.)

4 cups all-purpose flour
2 cups dried fruit, any kind add chopped nuts
1 cup honey
2 cups hot water
1 cup olive oil
2 teaspoons baking soda
1 teaspoon cloves
1 teaspoon nutmeg
1/4 teaspoon salt

Boil the fruit, honey olive the cloves, nutmeg, and salt for 5 minutes take off heat and let cool. Dissolve the soda in 1 tablespoon of water and pour into mixture and stir. Slowly stir in the flour. Pour into a greased cake pan and bake at 375oF for 45 minutes. This cake is not real sweet so you may desire to put an icing of some kind over it before serving.

A REAL SPONGE CAKE

There are many things a person can do with this basic cake. This recipe makes 2 - 9" round layers. This makes about 16 servings.

> 6 eggs, separated at room temperature, the whites in one bowl and the yolks in another.
> 1 cup all-purpose flour
> 1 cup honey
> 1/2 teaspoon salt
> 2 teaspoons vanilla

Beat egg yokes until thick, and slowly add the honey, salt, and vanilla, beating constantly with a whisk. Beat until very thick and the color of cream. If you are using a mixer, add in the flour very slowly at the slowest mixer speed. Beat the egg whites so little peaks form and fold into the batter a little at a time. Pour into 2 9" pie tins. Preheat the oven to 375oF and cook 25 minutes or until golden and springy. Cool in the pans about 10 minutes and then take out and let cool completely. Frost, as you desire.

DATE CAKE

Dates have been used for many centuries as a good food source in desert areas. In the last few hundred years it has been used for cakes. This recipe makes 8 servings.

2 cups of flour
1 cup sugar
1 cup hot water
1 cup chopped dates
1 cup chopped walnuts
1 cup mayonnaise
2 teaspoons baking soda
1 teaspoon vanilla

Pour the hot water over the dates, mix in the soda, let stand 5 minutes; then add the remaining ingredients and stir well. Bake in a well-greased and floured pan at 375oF for 30 minutes.

CARROT CAKE

I do not know where this was first made but I do know it is good. Makes 8 servings.

CAKE:

2 cups flour
2 cups grated carrots
2 cups brown sugar
3/4 cup olive oil
3 eggs
3/4 cup buttermilk
2 teaspoon cinnamon
2 teaspoon vanilla
1/2 teaspoon salt
2 teaspoon baking soda
1 small can crushed pineapple, drained
3-1/2 oz. coconut

Mix all the dry ingredients together, beat eggs, add oil, buttermilk, sugar and vanilla, mix carrots, coconut, and nuts. Pour into a pan 9 x 13 x 2-1/2". Bake for 55 minutes and bake at 375oF.

FROSTING:

- 1 cup sugar
- 1 cube butter
- 1/2 cup buttermilk
- 1 teaspoon white corn syrup
- 1/2 teaspoon soda
- 1 teaspoon vanilla

Mix sugar, buttermilk, butter, corn syrup, and soda in a saucepan. Boil 5 minutes. Remove from the heat; add the vanilla and pour hot over a hot cake. Use fairly large pan since this foams up.

NO NAME CAKE

I do not have a name for this cake but it is a cake. Makes 9 servings.

- 1-1/2 cups flour
- 1 cup of water
- 1 cup sugar
- 6 tablespoons of butter
- 1 teaspoon baking soda
- 1/2 cup cocoa
- 1 teaspoon vanilla

Mix the dry ingredients. Melt the butter and mix with vanilla, and water. Mix all items together and stir well until everything is moist. Bake 30 minutes at 350oF.

BREADS, ROLLS, BISCUITS, & BUNS

The smell of bread baking in your oven is one of the true joys of being a cook. There are two kinds of bread, good and better. Bread is served either cold or hot and I prefer mine hot. So, I will discuss hot breads first. There are breads that can be cooked as soon as the batter is completed and these are most often called "Short Breads." These short breads include rolls, biscuits, buns, muffins, popovers, pancakes, waffles, and most corn breads.

Yeast breads require time and attention to detail. Most breads that have yeast in them require a period for the yeast to work so these breads can not be cooked at once. Yeast is used to make leaven bread, the ingredients that are mixed with the yeast helps it grow because yeast is a living thing that needs, moisture, food, warmth and some times light to grow. There are many different textures to yeast breads because no two of them are made the same way or with the exact same ingredients. Both types of bread will be covered in some detail later in this chapter. In many parts of the world, the short breads are served hot or warm, and the yeast based breads are eaten cold.

When I was a boy, my mother made fresh bread two or three times a day. We had biscuits, pancakes or waffles for breakfast. We had hot bread for lunch and rolls for dinner. We did a lot of baking when I was a boy. We made cakes and pies often. My favorite bread is popovers but I start with biscuits because they are most likely to be served with wild game.

BUTTERMILK BISCUITS

If done correctly biscuits are light wonderful breads. This recipe will make about 18 biscuits. You can use either a white flour or a whole wheat flour when making these biscuits.

2 cups flour
1 tablespoon baking powder
1 teaspoon salt
1/3 cup shortening
2/3 cup buttermilk

Preheat the oven to 450oF. Mix the flour, baking powder, and salt together in a mixing bowl. Put the shortening and buttermilk into a blender with the dry ingredients and mix until the dough holds together. Knead gently on a lightly floured board 8 or 10 times. Roll the mixture until about 1/2" thick, then cut with a cookie cutter. Place on a baking sheet about 3/4" apart. For a glaze on top of the biscuits so they will glisten when finished, use melted butter. Bake about 15 minutes or until golden brown. Serve hot with lots of butter. Each biscuit is about 85 calories with out butter.

CORN BREAD

I do love corn bread and this recipe will make about 12 servings.

1-1/2 cups Yellow Corn Meal
1/2 cup all-purpose flour or wheat flour
1 tablespoon baking powder
1 teaspoon salt

4 tablespoons of honey
1 cup of milk
1/3 cup olive oil
1 egg

Combine the corn meal, flour, baking powder and salt in a mixing bowl. In another bowl mix the honey, milk, oil and egg, mix well. Mix the dry with the wet ingredients and stir until just blended. Into a greased 8 inch square pan, pour the mixture. Hold the pan about 3 inches above a hard surface and drop it 2 times it helps get the bubbles out of the mixture. Place into an oven that has been preheated to 400oF and bake about 20 to 25 minutes. Insert a wooden pick into the center of the pan and if it comes out clean, the bread is ready to serve. Serve warm. About 110 calories each without the butter.

MEXICAN CORN BREAD

This corn bread has a little more heat to it than the one above because of the chiles. This will make about 12 servings.

1-1/2 cups corn meal
1/2 cup all purpose flour or whole wheat flour
1 tablespoon baking powder
1 teaspoon salt
1 cup milk
1 egg
4 tablespoons melted butter
1/2 cup or 4 ounce can Ortega green chiles, diced
2 tablespoons diced pimento
1 cup frozen corn or can corn, drained
1/2 cup (2 ounces) cheddar cheese, shredded

Combine the corn meal, flour, baking powder, salt, and cheese in a bowl, mix very well. In another bowl mix the egg, milk and 4 tablespoons melted butter. In a medium skillet, put 1 tablespoon butter; add the chilies, pimento, and onion. Cook about 3 to 5 minutes, add the corn and cook for 2 minutes. Add the cooked vegetables and milk mixture to the flour and mix until just blended. Pour into a well-greased 8 inch pan. Hold the pan about 3 inches from a hard surface and drop it 2 times. This helps get the bubbles out. In an oven preheated to 400oF bake 35 to 40 minutes or until a wooden pick comes out clean.

BACON AND CORN MUFFINS

I love muffins with some power to them and with the bacon, these taste great. You can add many things to a corn muffin but I add bacon because I like the taste of bacon.

1-1/2 cups yellow corn meal
1/2 cup all purpose flour or wheat flour
1 tablespoon baking powder
1/2 teaspoon salt
1 cup milk
1 egg
3 tablespoons honey
1/2 cup fresh corn kernels or thawed frozen corn
6 slices of bacon, fried very crisp and cooled, then crumbled and set aside

In a mixing bowl, mix the corn meal, flour, baking powder and salt. In a different bowl, mist the milk, egg, honey and corn. Add the wet mixture to the dry ingredients and stir until blended. Into a buttered muffin tin, spoon the preparation and fill each cup about 2/3 full. Place the tin into a preheat oven to 400oF. Bake about 15 minutes or until a wooden toothpick inserted into a muffin comes out clean. Cool 3 to 4 minutes and remove. About 135 calories each without butter. Makes about 16 muffins.

POPOVERS

These are my favorite bread. They are light and served hot they are so wonderful. The are easy and quick to make and are so good.

1 Cup all purpose flour or wheat flour
1 cup of milk
2 eggs
2 tablespoons unsalted butter, melted
1/4 teaspoon salt

You may bake these in muffin tins or popover pans. The muffin size is most often used when dining on wild game. It is best to have all the ingredients ready, as popovers need to be baked just before serving.

Combine the eggs and salt in a bowl. Using a whisk stir in the milk and butter and then the flour until it is blended. Be very careful about the amount of butter you put into the mixture. Some people think more butter is better. Not in this bread. If you put more butter than indicated these will not popover they will fall and you will have 12 little cups with butter at the bottom. If this happens do not worry, you just turn them bottom up on the serving tray, they will be golden brown, and everyone will know you are a great cook.

It is best if you have two ovens to cook popovers but it can be done with one oven. If you have two ovens place the tin in a cold oven. Set the oven temperature to 425oF and bake 20 minutes. Reduce the heat to 375oF and bake about 12 to 15 minutes or until popovers are golden. They should be crisp. If you only have one oven, after you have taken out the wild game increase the heat to 425oF and bake as indicated above. Once these are ready open the oven and punch a tiny hole in the top of each one with an ice pick or small knife to let out the steam and put them back into the oven for 2 minutes. Makes about 12 popovers, about 85calories each.

YORKSHIRE PUDDING

Yorkshire Pudding has been served with wild game for hundreds of years. It was designed as a bread to be served with game and gravy. It must be served straight from the oven. It looks something like popovers but is very different. Both of these breads are full of steam when they come from the oven and a hole is punched in popovers to let the steam out but the steam is left in the pudding.

2 tablespoon melted game drippings
1/2 cup flour
1/2 teaspoon salt
1/4 cup water
1/2 cup milk
2 eggs, previously beaten

Mix salt and flour in bow, add the milk, beating as you pour. Add the water and eggs and beat. Cover the bowl and let stand in a cool place (not your refrigerator) about half an hour. After letting let stand beat a couple of minutes until bubbles appear. Into a muffin tin, pour a small amount of the wild game drippings. Put tin in oven and let it heat until it is smoking very lightly. Take out of oven and spoon in to each cup about 4 tablespoons batter put back in oven and cook 8-10 minutes or until rinsed and crisp. (DO NOT pierce with a knife as in the recipe above or the steam will come out and the puddings will collapse.) Put the puddings around the game and allow one pudding for each serving of game. Top with lots of hot gravy. About 90 calories per serving without the gravy.

FIG, WALNUT, PECAN BREAD

You may desire a bread with a hearty character and a firmness for some of the wild game you cook. The bread goes good with wonderful meat and a good red wine. This recipe makes one medium loaf and will serve 10 to 12 slices.

1 cup whole-wheat flour
1/2 cup all purpose flour
1/2 teaspoon baking powder
1/2 teaspoon salt
1-1/2 teaspoons baking soda
1/4 cup honey
2 cups dried figs, chopped very small
1/2 cup chopped walnuts
1/2 cup chopped pecans
2 eggs
1/4 cup unsalted butter at room temperature
1 cup boiling water

Preheat the oven to 350oF. Grease and flour a loaf pan. In a bowl, mix the two flours, the baking powder and the salt. In another bowl put in the figs, butter, and baking soda and pour the boiling water over them, stir well and let stand 15 minutes. Beat the honey walnuts and eggs into the fig mixture until all are blended. Then put the flour mixture into the figs and mix well. Pour all this into the loaf pan. Hold the pan 3 inches from a hard surface and drop 2 times to take out the bubbles. Bake about 55 to 65 minutes depending on your oven. In my oven, it takes 50 minutes on the lower shelf. Put a toothpick in and if it comes out clean, it is done. Let cool a while before serving. Makes 1 loaf. Thin slices are about 150 calories each.

WHOLE WHEAT MUFFINS

This recipe makes 12 muffins

- 1-1/4 cups whole wheat flour
- 1/2 cup all purpose flour
- 1 tablespoon baking powder
- 1 teaspoon salt
- 1 cup milk
- 1/4 cup olive oil
- 4 tablespoons molasses
- 1 egg

Combine the flours, baking powder and salt in a bowl. Then mix the milk, oil, molasses, and egg in another bowl, mix completely. Make a well in the center of the dry ingredients and pour in the liquids and mix. Stop mixing when the batter is lumpy. Spoon into your greased muffin tin filling each cup about 2/3rd. In a preheated oven at 425oF bake about 20-25 minutes or until brown. Serve hot. About 140 calories per muffin (without the butter).

IRISH SODA BREAD

In Ireland, they have been making this bread for centuries. It is usually made with whole wheat flour rather than white. It is most often made with no butter or margarine. When you are serving this cut it in small slices not wedges. This will make a 6" round.

- 4 cups of whole wheat flour
- 2 teaspoons baking soda
- 1-1/2 teaspoons salt
- 1/4 cup olive oil
- 1-2/3 cups buttermilk or sour milk

Into a large mixing bowl, pour the flour, soda, salt, and mix. Then pour in the olive oil and the milk and mix until the texture is course. On a lightly floured board, knead until smooth, about 5 - 7 minutes. Shape into a round loaf about 6" across. Cut a cross in the top about 1/2" deep and dust in a little flour. Place in a well greased dish and bake in oven at 400oF for about 40 - 50 minutes or until it has a hard, golden crust. Turn the loaf upside down on a wire rack and let cool. Makes about 20 slices of 110 calories each.

BOSTON CAN BREAD

This bread is made in a can sitting upright on a rack. This bread is not baked it is steamed. The size can to use is about 4" across the top and about 7" tall. If you do not have or can not find the cans, you may use molds.

- 1-1/2 cups whole wheat flour
- 1 cup all purpose flour
- 1 teaspoon salt
- 1 teaspoon baking soda
- 1 teaspoon baking powder
- 1/2 cup corn meal
- 2 cups buttermilk
- 1 cup raisins
- 3/4 cup molasses

Mix the flours, salt, soda, baking powder and corn meal. Mix the buttermilk, molasses and raisins and pour into the flour and mix. If you have cans, line the bottoms with greased wax paper. If you have molds do the same thing. Pour in the mixture until the can or the mold is 2/3rd full. Put greased foil over the top of the can and tie or tape very securely. In a large kettle or pot place a rack, put the cans on the rack, and put in boiling water to come halfway up on the cans, cover and steam about one hour or until risen. Insert a small sharp knife into the middle of the can and if it comes out clean, the bread is done. Take the cans out of the kettle and let cook a few minutes then turn the cans upside down and the bread will fall out. Lay bread on side and cut into slices about 1/4" thick. Each slice about 90 calories.

YEAST BREADS

Yeast breads take much longer to make than the quick breads detailed in the previous pages. The ingredients you mix with the yeast are very important for they help the yeast do its work. Yeast is a tiny living fungus that requires moisture, warmth, food, air and sweetness and salt to work. Yeast produces gases that makes the bread rise. Flour is the most important part of yeast bread for it provides the (gluten), protein that develops in the stretching and kneading, as the yeast grows, and it sets during the baking process. These are the things that give each yeast bread its texture. All purpose flour is called for in all of these recipes for it is the best for yeast breads. The whole wheat flour in the previous recipes does not yield a good loaf nor does cake or pastry flour which is too soft for good bread of this type. Milk or water is used as the liquids to make yeast bread. The water will give the bread a crisper crust, (like in French bread) a chewier texture, and a nuttier flavor. Milk will increase the food value and keeping quality. Olive oil, butter, margarine, shortening, or lard may be used in making yeast bread. Different products give off different flavors and you should use the flavor you like best. The fat in the bread improves the keeping quality, aids in browning and gives it the fine texture.

Salt is used in all these breads and it is not just for flavor. The action of the yeast is controlled by the salt. The correct amount keeps the dough from rising too fast, but too much salt slows the rising of the dough. Sugar is a food for people but is also a food that yeast needs sugar also help the browning process.

Mixing is very important. All the ingredients should be vigorously and thoroughly mixed so the yeast is evenly distributed. You can use an electric beater or wooden spoon for this process. As the dough is mixed it will form a ball in the middle of the bowl. After mixing, the dough must be kneaded. After mixing put the dough on a lightly dusted board. Knead for about 3 minutes and then let stand about 10 minutes, then start kneading again. Knead for about 10 minutes. If you are called away with a phone call or interrupted for more than 10 minutes, put a damp towel over the dough so it will not dry out.

When you set the dough aside to rise you should not shake the bowl or disturb it in any way. This is the time the gas is released from the yeast that causes the stretching of the gluten that makes the dough rise. The time required will be different in every bread and in every location. The dough should be in a warm place and the first rising will take about two or more hours. It will take longer in a cool kitchen or if there is no sugar in the mixture. The second rising will last about one-half hour and then when you put it into the pans, that rising will last about and hour or less.

The one thing about homemade bread is that each loaf is very different from the last. You may make the loafs in any shape you desire. Some round, some long, some short, etc. You can make a French loaf, braids, pan rolls, cloverleaf rolls, rings, or any thing you desire. With this dough, you can make croissants, Danish pastry, Parker house rolls or fan-tans.

Baking kills the action of the yeast. Properly baked the bread is nice and brown and will slide out of the pan easily.

There are always problems with baking at home. In the yeast, breads there are five basic difficulties to face and they are:

1. Dry and heavy bread: too much flour, follow the recipe
2. Lopsided loaves: An unlevel rack in an oven or pans may be touching the oven walls or one another.
3. Crumbly bread: It took too long to rise after shaping.
4. Small doughy loves are caused by a rising that was too long or too short, or too much or too little heat.
5. Breads that are yeasty or sour are caused by too much heat during the rising process.

FAMILY WHITE BREAD

This is a delicious bread that is simple for anyone. If you have not made yeast bread before this is where you start.

6 Cups of all-purpose flour
2 teaspoons salt

3 tablespoons honey
1/2 cup milk
3 tablespoons melted butter
1-1/2 cups warm water (105oF)
1 package active dry yeast

Heat 1 cup of water, add in the milk, salt, honey, and let stand until lukewarm. In another bowl place 1/2 cup of water and heat, stir in the yeast and let stand for 5 minutes to dissolve. Mix the two bowls together, add butter and the flour a little at a time and stir well. Turn out onto a lightly floured board and knead for about 10 minutes or until satiny and elastic. You may add a little flour if desired. Shape into a ball, put in a large bowl, and put olive oil in bowl. Roll until all surfaces of the ball are covered. Cover with a damp towel and let stand about an hour or until the dough has doubled in size. Pour the dough out on lightly floured board and let set 5 minutes, knead 3 minutes. Cut in half and form 2 loves about 8" x 4". Put in greased loaf pans and let sit about one hour or until size of dough has doubled. Preheat oven to 375oF and bake bread about 45 minutes or until brown. Take out of oven and tap with a kitchen knife, the loaf should sound hollow. Turn out of pans and place on cooling rack. About 90 calories per slice.

WESTERN SOUR DOUGH

This bread takes 2 to 3 days to make so you must start it days before it is to be used. No short cuts for this bread, but it is worth the wait. It makes 2 long, narrow loaves or 2 rounds.

(NOTE: On the ranches of the Western United States we keep some of this going all the time as we use it to make sour dough pancakes).

Sour Dough Starter:

- 1 Cup all purpose flour
- 1 Cup cold water
- 1 Tablespoon sugar

Two days before you need this you must start the preparation. In a mixing bow, mix the flour and water until smooth and pour into a 1-quart glass jar, then add the sugar and stir until it is completely dissolved. Cover loosely and let stand in a warm (about 80oF) until the mixture ferments, it will bubble and smell sour. Stir from time to time during the fermenting process.

Bread:

- 5 cups all purpose flour
- 1 tablespoon of sugar
- 1 tablespoon salt
- 1 cup of the sour dough starter
- 1 package active dry yeast
- 1 cup warm water (105oF)

Mix the flour, sugar and salt and sit aside. Pour warm water into a bowl, break the yeast into the water, stir and dissolve. Mix the starter with the flour mix, a little at a time. Put on lightly floured board and knead about 10 minutes or until elastic. Put in a bowl and grease all over. Cover with a damp towel and let sit about one hour or until the dough has doubled in size. You may make round bread or long loaves. If you make long loaves place on a cookie sheet and let rest until they have doubled in size. You should preheat the oven to 400oF. Brush the tops of the loaves with cold water and make a cut in them if you desire. Bake on the top shelf of the oven and on the lower shelf place a pan half full of water. Cook 40 to 45 minutes or until brown and sound hollow when tapped. Cool on a rack before cutting. About 70 calories each.

DARK RYE BREAD

Rye bread has been around for many centuries and is widely used in Eastern Europe. The recipe makes a medium dark loaf. (NOTE: Rye flour will be a bit sticky even after being thoroughly kneaded). The recipe makes 2 loaves.

3 cups rye flour
3 cups whole wheat flour
1 tablespoon salt
2 tablespoons dark-brown sugar
2 tablespoons olive oil
2 packages dry yeast
1 cup milk
1 cup water

In 1/2 cup of war water break in the yeast and let stand for 5 minutes. Bring 1 cup of water to a boil, mix in the salt, sugar, olive oil and milk, and let stand until lukewarm. Add the two items together and pour in the rye flour, stirring all the time. Add in enough of the wheat flour to make the dough correct. Turn out onto a lightly floured breadboard and knead for 2 minutes, let it rest for 10 minutes. Start kneading again and do that about 10 minutes. You may add additional flour as needed. Put the dough in a greased bowl and cover the entire ball with grease... Cover and place in a warm place until the size has doubled. Shape into to two loaves. Place in loaf pans and cook at 400oF for 40 - 50 minutes. Remove when cooked and let cool.

AMERICAN STYLE FRENCH BREAD

French bread in France and French bread in America are very different breads. In America it is a long thin loaf, crisp on the outside and soft on the inside and is often used as a dinner bread.
This recipe makes two 15" loaves.

6 cups all purpose flour
2 tablespoons sugar
1 egg
4 tablespoons olive oil
2 packages dry yeast
2 cups water

In 2 cups of warm water, stir in the years and let stand for 5 minutes to dissolve. Add into this the sugar, oil and stir well. Add in 5 cups of the flour and mix thoroughly. Pour out onto a lightly floured board and knead a few minutes then let rest for 10 minutes. Start kneading again and add the remaining flour so the mixture is no longer sticky and is elastic and very smooth. Place in a greased bowl and cover with grease; let stand in a warm place until the ball has doubled in size. Take out of bowl and knead a few time then shape into long 15" loaves. Place on a greased cookie sheet and let stand until they have again doubled in size. Preheat oven to 400oF. To glaze the top before baking, beat the egg into a tablespoon of water and add 1 tablespoon of salt, brush this mixture over the top of the loaves. Bake about 40 - 50 minutes. About 110 calories per slice.

SALADS , GREENAND BUNNY FOOD

There are three basic kinds of salads. The green leafy salad based on lettuce, cabbage, etc., the vegetable salad and the fruit salad. These can be mixed in a thousand different ways. Many times, there are meats of different kinds placed on the top of the lettuce or other greens.

When I was a boy in Texas, we always had the salad before the meal. However, many people have salads at many different times in a meal. In France the salad can come before or after the main course, in Russia the salad is usually the last item in the meal. In the Southern part of the United States on a hot summer night, a frozen fruit salad will be served at the end of the meal rather than a dessert.

The standard lettuce in the United States is a firm head of iceberg lettuces. Now there are dozens of different types of lettuce. In the average supermarket, you can purchase prepackaged lettuce with many different types of lettuce in the same package. These are usually cut, washed and packaged so all one has to do when you get them home is to run a little cold water over the item.

Other types of lettuce are named, Bibb, Boston, Butter-head, Cos, Leaf, Romaine, and Simpson. Other type of greens used in salads are: Beet greens, Belgian Endive, Cabbage, Chicory, Chinese Cabbage, Corn Salad (also known as Field Salad), Curly Endive, Dandelions, Dock greens, Escarole, Garden Cress, Mustard greens, Nasturtium, Peppergrass, Rugula, Sorrel, Turnip Greens, and Watercress.

SALAD DRESSINGS

There are two basic types of salad dressings, and a thousand different ways to mix the dressings. The two types are those made with oil and vinegar or those based on yogurt or mayonnaise. The most common perhaps is a mixture of oil and vinegar. Since you use very little vinegar, this is called vinaigrette, which is French for "little vinegar." The most simple is to used lemon juice which does not add a much acidity as the vinegar. You may use either red wine or white wine vinegar. The red wine will give off a slightly hearty flavor than the white wine.

BASIC VINAIGRETTE

Covers about one pound of greens and serves 6 persons.

1/4 cup extra virgin olive oil
1 tablespoon of wine vinegar
Salt and pepper to taste

Mix in a small bowl; pour over green and toss.

HERB VINAIGRETTE

Same ingredients as above, add the herbs you like.

WESTERN VINAIGRETTE

Same Ingredients as Basic but add 3 cloves of garlic, 1 tablespoon of honey.

MAYONNAISE OR YOGURT DRESSINGS

May I suggest you purchase a good quality mayonnaise at the supermarket rather than make you own. If you desire to make your own mayonnaise, you make it two to three days before the big meal and store in the refrigerator. Remember in making your own mayonnaise takes time and there is a lot of clean up after you finish. It is easier to buy the mayonnaise. To make one cup of mayonnaise do the following.

1 cup extra virgin olive oil
1 egg yolk
2 tablespoons fresh lemon juice
Salt and pepper to taste.
1 teaspoon mustard (only if you like mustard a lot)

Place the lemon juice, and egg yolk in a food processor with a beater blade, start the motor and pour the oil in very slowly until the blend is smooth.

SALADS, GREENS AND BUNNY FOODS!

SMIPLE ICEBERG

A very common lettuce to use in a salad is the iceberg head. Peal off the unusable leaves and discard, with a very sharp knife cut out the stem and hold the head bottom up under a cold stream of water. Wash, drain, dry and put in refrigerator. If the salad is to be made soon, tear the leaves apart and dry, put on paper towel in refrigerator for a few minutes. Break the leaves into bite size pieces and put in salad bowl. About two cups per person pour the dressing you desire over the leaves in very small amounts. More is not better here. Add such other items, as you may desire to complete the salad.

(Note) When I was a boy, we cut a head of iceberg into four pieces. Each person received one forth of the head and we always had Thousand Island dressing over it because my Mother liked to make her own Thousand Island dressing.

WILTED LETTUCE

A favorite at my house was wilted lettuce salad, my Mother was a master at making it and I have included it in this book at the request of my niece. (NOTE: When we cooked bacon for breakfast, we cooked more than we needed and set it aside a room temperature but covered. We saved the bacon fat in a quart jar in the refrigerator.) This recipe makes 6 servings.

1-1/2 quart salad greens
1/2 cup minced scallions

6 slices of bacon
Salt and pepper to taste
2 tablespoons apple cider vinegar
1 teaspoon sugar

Fry the bacon, if you have not previously done so. Drain, crumble and set aside. Take 4 tablespoons of dripping from skillet or from your reserve; mix in the salt, pepper, sugar, and vinegar and heat. When simmering, pour over greens and add the bacon, scallions, and if you like sliced hard boiled eggs, toss and serve at once.

CAESAR SALAD

This may be the most popular salad served in America. It is on the menu of almost ever restaurant in one form or other.

1 large head romaine lettuce, washed and crisped
2 cups 1/2" bread cubes (you can make you own or purchase at supermarket)
2/3 cup extra virgin olive oil
1/3 cup grated Parmesan cheese
2 cloves of garlic, peeled
1 raw egg
4 tablespoons of lemon juice
8 anchovy fillets, minced

Crush the garlic and mix with the oil and let stand overnight in a covered bowl at room temperature. Just before you are to make the salad pour the oil off and discard the garlic. Into the mixing bowl with the oil in it, add the egg and lemon juice and stir. Pour mixture over the lettuce and toss; add cheese, anchovies, salt and pepper toss again.

GREEN SALAD WITH FRUIT

Makes 6 servings

10 oz (1 package) of salad greens
1 cup apple cut into bite size pieces
1 cup slice strawberries
1 can (11oz) mandarin orange segments, drained
2 tablespoons sliced green onions

Place greens into individual plates and top with strawberry slices, orange segments, and sprinkle with apple and greens. Drizzle with Basic Vinaigrette, serve.

VENISON AND CELERY SALAD WITH WALNUTS

Makes 6 servings

1 head romaine lettuce, shredded
1 bunch celery
6 oz roasted venison, cut into long, thin strips
1/2 cup walnuts, chopped
5 tablespoons extra-virgin olive oil
Juice from 1/2 lemon

Cut only the best of the celery into thin slices, cutting crosswise; toss with the lettuce and the venison. In a small bowl, mix the oil, lemon juice, walnuts, salt and pepper to taste. Pour over the lettuce and venison and toss again.

SIMPLE GREEN SALAD

Makes 6 servings

1 large handful of iceberg lettuce
4 endive (red or green)
1 large handful of romaine
1 bell pepper, seeded, and chopped fine
1 cucumber, peeled and sliced thin
1 bunch, small green onions, cleaned and chopped

Cut the bottom off the endive and discard, clean and cross cut. Mix greens and pour peppers, onions, and cucumber over the lettuce. Use salad dressing of your choice, toss and serve.

COLESLAW

Makes 6 servings

2 quarts of grated cabbage
1/4 cup grated onion
2 carrots, peeled and grated
1/2 cup sour cream
2 tablespoons vinegar
Salt and pepper to taste

Mix the sour cream and vinegar, salt and pepper. In a large mixing bowl, place the cabbage, onion and carrots; pour the sour cream over this and toss well. Put in refrigerator, covered, let chill about 3 hours.

NASTURTIUM SALAD

Makes 6 servings.

1 quart mixed salad greens

1 pint nasturtium leaves, washed and dried
1 tablespoon minced parsley
1 teaspoon minced fresh marjoram
1 small bunch onions, washed, dried finely chopped

Mix all items together and use Western Vinaigrette or a salad dressing of your choice.

ANTELOPE AND SPINACH SALAD

Makes 6 servings

16 ounces of roasted or BBQ antelope
1 package spinach leaves, wash, stem and tare
4 thin slices of red onion, chopped
1/2 cup of Western Vinaigrette
1/4 cup crumbled blue cheese
2 tablespoons toasted walnuts

Wash and dry the spinach, mix with onions, and set aside. Take piece of antelope about one inch thick and about 4" across the top and about 8" long. Cut into pieces about 1"x4" by 1/2" thick. In a small sauce pan bring the vinaigrette to a boil and pour over spinach and onions; toss to coat. Put on plates, and arrange the antelope, sprinkle with walnuts and the blue cheese, serve.

RUSSIAN SALAD

Makes 6 servings

1 head romaine lettuce or lettuce of your choice
1 cup cold cooked beets, dices
1 cup cold cooked green peas
1 cup cold cooked cut green beans

1 cup cold cooked potatoes, diced
1 cup cold cooked carrots, diced
1/3 mayonnaise
1/3 cup French dressing
1 tablespoon capers

Mix all ingredients with the French dressing except the beets. Chill two hours then drain, saving the dressing. Add the beets and mayonnaise to the vegetables and toss well. Put the lettuce leaves on a plate and pour the vegetables over the leaves; sprinkle with capers.

GERMAN POTATOS SALAD

This salad can be served hot or cold. At my house, we usually serve it hot when serving wild game. Makes 6 servings.

6 medium-size boiled potatoes, peeled and cubed
6 hard cooked eggs, peeled and diced
1 cup coarsely chopped celery
1/2 cup minced green pepper
1/2 cup minced onion
1 tablespoon flour
3/4 cup cold water
1/4 cup vinegar
2 tablespoon sugar
1/4 teaspoon pepper
2 teaspoons salt
4 slices cooked bacon, crumbled

Put potatoes, green pepper, celery and onion into a large bowl and toss. In a small saucepan mix the flour, water, vinegar, sugar, and salt; bring to a boil and pour over the potatoes, etc.

Slice the eggs and arrange on top of the salad. With wild game, serve while everything is hot.

AVOCADO AND BROCCOLI SALAD

This is a salad that is often served with game. Makes 6 servings.

1 (good) avocado, do not cut until just before use
2 lbs. tender broccoli
1/4 cup chopped pecans
1/4 cup chopped walnuts
1/4 cup extra virgin olive oil
1 tablespoon minced fresh parsley
2 tablespoons lemon juice

Cut the broccoli from the large stems. Fill one saucepan with salted water and bring to a boil. In a mixing bowl put two cups of ice and fill half way up with water. To the boiling water add the broccoli and boil until tender, about 3 to 4 minutes. Take off heat and drain then pour drained broccoli at once into the ice water. This will retain the bright green color of the broccoli; otherwise, it turns white or pale gray. Cut the avocado into cubes and toss with lemon juice to prevent the avocado turning black. Toss the avocado, broccoli, olive oil, parsley, and lemon juice together, put in plates and sprinkle nuts over the mixture.

WILD FOWL SALAD

This salad is very popular in Western Europe where it is used with duck and other wild fowl. This make 6 servings.

4 large oranges

1 red onion, cut into very thin slices
12 black olives
1/2 cup extra virgin olive oil
1 teaspoon fresh oregano
Salt and pepper to taste

Put the onion in a bowl of cold water for 30 minutes before you need it. This will give the onion a milder flavor. Peel and cut the white membranes from the oranges while removing the seeds. Cut crosswise, arrange on plates, and put onion slices on top. Mix salt, pepper, oregano and olive oil and drizzle over oranges. Put in refrigerator until ready to serve.

CRAYFISH SALAD

This salad is most often seen in the Southern part of the United States. Makes 6 servings.

20 crayfish
3 large boiling potatoes
3 eggs, boiled, peeled and diced
Salt and pepper to taste
1/2 cup Western Vinaigrette or dressing of your choice

Remove the meat from the crayfish and put into salted boiling water. Boil the potatoes in the jackets and peel when they are cool and dice. After the crayfish are cooked, drain and add to the potatoes, eggs, and salad dressing, salt and pepper to taste.

ASPARAGUS WITH MOOSE OR BEAR

This is very common in France and Italy and in many other countries. Makes 6 servings.

1 lb. asparagus
3 cups of diced cooked moose or bear
1 head lettuce
2 hard boiled eggs
2 large tomatoes
Salt and pepper to taste

On 6 plates take 6 large lettuce leave and put one on each plate and set in refrigerator. Put a tied bunch of asparagus in salted, boiling water, with 1 teaspoon of sugar and boil about 30 minutes. Drain, cool, cut into bit size pieces and arrange on lettuce. Decorate each plate with sliced hard boiled eggs and tomato wedges, use a dressing of your choice, salt and pepper to taste.

GOOSE OR DUCK SALAD

This salad has been around for hundreds of years and can be made in many different ways. Makes 6 servings.

3 cups boneless cooked goose, diced
1 head of lettuce
6 pitted, spiced plums, diced
2 hard boiled eggs, sliced
1 apple, peeled and diced
1 cup cooked peas (frozen or canned)
1 large tomato cut into wedges
3/4 cup mayonnaise
Salt and pepper to taste

Toss all ingredients except the tomato and eggs. Mount on lettuce leaves and decorate with eggs and tomatoes.

PEARS CHARDONNAY

This is a very good cool salad. Serves 6.

6 large pears, pitted, peeled and cut into long slices
1 cup confectioners' sugar
3 cups Chardonnay (a good one)

In a bowl, mix the sugar and the Chardonnay; pour over the pears and chill an hour before serving.

B

BIRDS ON THE WING

CAJUN STYLE WHOLE FRIED TURKEY, 181
CLASSIC BRAISED DUCK, 179
DUTCH OVEN SIMMERED SESAME DUCK WITH SAUCE, 173
GAME BIRD WITH ONION, BACON AND MUSHROOMS, 177
QUAIL WITH CHERRY SAUCE, 176
ROAST GOOSE OR DUCK, 175
ROSEMARY BRAISED QUAIL, 180
SAUTED PHEASANT WITH RED WINE CREAM SAUCE, 178
STUFFED OVEN ROASTED CANADIAN HOLIDAY WILD GOOSE, 185
STUFFED PHEASANT, 174
WILD PRAIRIE HEN WITH CRANBERRY GLAZE, 182
WOOD SMOKED DUCK BREAST BACON WRAPPED, IN BLUSH WINE SAUCE, 184

BREADS, ETC.

AMERICAN STYLE FRENCH BREAD, 245
BACON AND CORN MUFFINS, 233, 234
BOSTON CAN BREAD, 238
BUTTERMILK BISCUITS, 231
CORN BREAD, 231
DARK RYE BREAD, 244
FAMILY WHITE BREAD, 242
FIG, WALNUT, PECAN BREAD, 236
IRISH SODA BREAD, 238
MEXICAN CORN BREAD, 232
WESTERN SOUR DOUGH, 243
WHOLE WHEAT MUFFINS, 237
YEAST BREADS, 239
YORKSHIRE PUDDING, 235

D

DESSERT SAUCES

BLUEBERRY AND GRAND MARNIER COULIS, 109
FRUIT COULIS FOR DESSERTS, 108
ORANGE BOURBON WHISKEY SAUCE, 109

DESSERTS

A REAL SPONGE CAKE, 226
APPLE PIE, 215
APPLESAUCE CAKE, 224
BASIC OIL PIE CRUST, 214
BASIC PIE CRUST WARM, 212, 213
BEST CHOCOLATE CAKE, 221
BRANDIED MINCEMEAT PIE, 220
CARL'S PECAN PIE, 218
CARROT CAKE, 227
CHOCOLATE BUNDT CAKE, 223
DATE CAKE, 227
FRESH FRUIT PIES, 216
FRESH RHUBARB PIE, 219
KEY LIME PIE, 220
NO NAME CAKE, 228
OATMEAL CAKE, 224
PUMPKIN PIE, 217
SPICE CAKE, 225

F

FISH & OTHERS
BAKED STUFFED FISH, 161
BLACKENED FISH WITH CREOLE SAUCE, 162
CAJUN FRIED FISH, 161
FROGS LEGS SCAMPI STYLE, 166
GRILLED ALLIGATOR TAIL STEAKS, 165
GRILLED SMOKED FROG, 167
LEMON BAKED FISH, 156
MISSISSIPPI STYLE BUTTERMILK CATFISH, 158
PAN FRIED PIKE, 157
RAINBOW TROUT POACHED IN WHITE WINE AND DILL, 168
TRADITIONAL ALLIGATOR STEW, 164
TROUT ALMANDINE A LA GRILL, 160

L

LARGE GAME
ANTELOPE KABOBS WITH POLYNESSIAN SAUCE, 143
BOAR CHOPS WITH MUSHROOMS AND PEPPERS, 150
BROILED BEAR STEAKS WITH SPICY MUSTARD MARINADE, 146
GLAZED CARIBOU SHORT RIBS, 149
GRILLED BUFFALO T-BONE STEAKS WITH GARLIC COMPOUND OR MATER D' BUTTER, 140
GRILLED SMOKED VENISON CHOPS WITH JALAPENO BEURRE BLANC SAUCE, 133
GUINNESS MARINADED ELK STEAKS, 137
HERB SAVORY BEAR STEAKS, 148
OVEN ROASTED LEG OF RAM WITH ROSEMARY AND HERB BEARNAISE SAUCE, 145
RED WINE MARINATED MOOSE ROAST WITH CRACKED BLACK PEPPER SAUCE, 142
ROASTED ELK WITH A MUSHROOM AND ONION BURGANDY SAUCE, 138
ROASTED LOIN OF VENISON WITH ROSEMARY AND THYME, 135
ROASTED VENISON WITH SHERRY & SAUTEED RED ONION SAUCE, 132
SEARED RAM CHOPS WITH LIME & GINGER SAUCE, 144
SLOW SMOKED VENISON BRISKET WITH HONEY BAR-B-QUE SAUCE, 136
TEXAS STYLE VENISON FAJITAS, 134
TRADITIONAL BUFFALO ROAST, 141
WHISKEY SOAKED SADDLE OF BOAR, 151

M

MARINADE

BASIC BURGANDY RED MARINADE, 50
BASIC SEASONED BUTTERMILK SOAK, 46
BASIC WHITE WINE MARINADE, 50
CHILI PEPPER TEXAS MARINADE, 48
HOT & WILD CHILI & SOY MARINADE FOR FISH, 53
LEMON & LIME MARINADE FOR FISH, 53
MARINADE FOR LARGE GAME, 54
SIPPIN WHISKEY MARINADE, 52
SOUTHERN STYLE "RED NECK" GAME MARINADE, 47
SWEET MILK MARINADE FOR VENISON, 51
TANGY CITRUS MARINADE, 49
TART VINEGAR SOAK/MARINADE, 47

R

RUBS

CARIBBEAN PASTE OR DAMP RUB, 68
CHIPOLTIE PEPPER DAMP RUB, 65
DRY MARINADE FOR FISH, 66
FALL HARVEST APPLE AND PEAR DAMP RUB, 62
HUNTERS SPICE AND HERB DRY RUB (SEASONED SALT), 63
JERK DRY RUB SEASONING, 67
KICK BUTT SOUTH OF THE BOARDER RUB, 61
LARGE GAME STIR FRY DAMP RUB, 71
OLD LOUISIANNA STYLE DAMP RUB FOR FISH, 69
QUICK & SIMPLE DRY RUB, 60
SOUTHEAST ASIAN HOT & WILD DAMP RUB, 70
TANGY SWEET MUSTARD DAMP RUB, 64

S

SALADS

ANTELOPE AND SPINACH SALAD, 254
ASPARAGUS WITH MOOSE OR BEAR, 258
AVOCADO AND BROCCOLI SALAD, 256
BASIC VINAIGRETTE, 248
CAESAR SALAD, 251
COLESLAW, 253
CRAYFISH SALAD, 257
GERMAN POTATOS SALAD, 255
GOOSE OR DUCK SALAD, 258
GREEN SALAD WITH FRUIT, 252
HERB VINAIGRETTE, 248
MAYONNAISE OR YOGURT DRESSINGS, 249
NASTURTIUM SALAD, 254
PEARS CHARDONNAY, 259
RUSSIAN SALAD, 255
SIMPLE GREEN SALAD, 253
SMIPLE ICEBERG, 250
VENISON AND CELERY SALAD WITH WALNUTS, 252
WESTERN VINAIGRETTE, 249
WILD FOWL SALAD, 257
WILTED LETTUCE, 250

SAUCES, GRAVIES, VINAIGRETTES AND TOPPERS

ANY CHEF'S BASIC VINAIGRETTE, 97
AVOCADO RELISH, 102
BASIC RED WINE VINAIGRETTE WITH GARLIC & ONION, 100
BASIC ROUX: WHITE, BLONDE & BROWN, 90
CHILLED HORSERADISH CHUTNEY, 106
CILANTRO & LIME VINIAGRETTE, 98
COMPOUND BUTTER FOR ANY OCCASION, 92
CRACKED BLACK PEPPER SAUCE, 103
FAR-EAST ORIENTAL VINAIGRETTE, 99
FRESH PESTO BUTTER, 93
GINGER AND LIME SAUCE, 104
HONEY BAR-B-QUE SAUCE, 104
MANGO CHUTNEY FOR GRILLED FISH, 101
ROSEMARY HERB SAUCE, 105
SIMPLE POLYNESIAN SAUCE, 107
SOUTHWESTERN PICO De GALLO, 102
SPICY CREOLE MUSTARD BUTTER, 96
STEAK BUTTER OR "MAITRE d' BUTTER", 95
TRADITIONAL ALMOND BUTTER, 94
TRADITIONAL GARLIC & CHIVE BUTTER, 94
VINAIGRETTE WITH SUN-DRIED TOMATOES, 98
WILD MUSTANG GRAPE AND PECAN CHUTNEY, 106

SIDE DISHES

ASPARAGUS WITH LEMON-BALSAMIC VINAIGRETTE, 207
BABY CARROTS SAUTED WITH PEPPERS, MUSHROOMS, AND GARLIC, 199
BROCCOLI WITH ROASTED PEPPERS AND OLIVES, 205
DOWN HOME VENISON RED BEANS AND RICE, 195
GRILLED EGGPLANT WITH GINGER BUTTER, 201
JALAPENO & LIME MARINATED GRILLED VEGETABLES WITH PEPPER SAUCE, 199
LEMON SAUTED SPINICH AND GREENS WITH SESAME SEEDS, 206
LOUISIANA PECAN "DIRTY RICE", 196
OVEN BROILED TOMATOES WITH GARLIC, FETA & OLIVES, 202
PAN SAUTED CHILI POTATOES WITH MIXED PEPPERS, 192
PAN SAUTED GREEN BEANS WITH ROSEMARY, ALMONDS AND MUSHROOMS., 208
PAN SAUTED, BALSAMIC & HERB GARDEN BLEND VEGETABLES, 209
ROASTED RED GARLIC POTATOES WITH SAUTED MUSHROOMS & ROSEMARY, 191
ROASTED VEGETABLES WITH APPPLE WINE SAUCE, 207
SEASONED FRIED ZUCCHINI WITH PEPPER AND

TOMATO VINAIGRETTE, 203
SOURDOUGH APPLE-SAGE DRESSING WITH ALMONDS, 197
SWEET POTATOES WITH APPLES AND A MAPLE-PECAN GLAZE, 190
SWEET POTATOES WITH CRANBERRY GLAZE, 189
WILD GAME STOCK RICE PILALF, 193

SMALL GAME

BAKED RACCOON, 121
BURGANDY PAN SAUTED SQUIRREL WITH MUSHROOMS, 115
DIJON BAR-B-QUED WOODCHUCK, 123
HASENPFEFFER, 118
HONEY GLAZED SQUIRREL WITH GINGER, 113
LONE STAR DEEP FRIED RATTLESNAKE with AVOCADO RELISH, 122
LOUISIANNA CREOLE RABBIT WITH SPICY CREOLE SAUCE, 119
OVEN BAKED MUSKRAT IN A RED WINE, GARLIC AND BASIL TOMATO SAUCE WITH PENNE PASTA, 125
PAN SEARED BEAVER CUTLETS WITH PEPPER MUSHROOM SAUCE, 126
RABBIT VIN BLANC, 117
SOUTHERN SMOKED SQUIRREL WITH PECANS, 116
SOUTHWEST MESIQUTE BAR-B-QUED JAVALINA, 127

STOCKS

BASIC AND UNIVERSAL VEGETABLE STOCK, 82
BASIC BOUILLON RECIPE, WITH WINE VARIATIONS, 83
BASIC GAME BROWN STOCK, 79
BASIC GAME FISH STOCK, 81
BASIC WHITE GAME STOCK, 78